Georgie

A teenage memoir

George Burton

ISBN 978-0-9927889-2-6

Published by Kelsoprint

Printed by Createspace

Acknowledgements

My sincere thanks to the following who gave permission to use their photographs:

D C Thomson Ltd

Douglas Bryce

Dundee City Archives

Evening Telegraph

Jaques of London

Jean-Luc François

Karen Gray

Libraries, Leisure and Culture Dundee

Nationaal Archief NL

One Voice Volunteer Group

Renée Rapa

Retro Dundee

Ricky Gierelo

Special thanks to my brother Joe Burton, who edited this book as well as starring in it alongside the author.

This book is dedicated to Frank & Peggy,

my wonderful parents.

1

Limbo

The year was 1965 and George Gerard Burton had just turned 12 years old.

Like the City of Dundee itself, my little world was in a state of change where old certainties were being challenged and new prospects were being revealed. Our move out to Charleston from the crumbling town centre tenements had definitely improved our quality of life, but my Dad still had to work every hour God sent to put food on the table for Mum, Joe and myself. Luckily for me, my folks knew that education was the only sure way out of poverty for ordinary people like us, and normally I was a very happy boy at home and at school.

At the end of February we all left Mrs. Balbirnie and St. Mary's Lochee primary school behind. Most of us were truly sad to be leaving a place where we felt safe and cared for, and where we'd been shown the way to be good citizens and good people. That's with the obvious exception of my pal Walter who had learned everything he'd set out to learn, even though the skills he had acquired weren't exactly those defined in the primary school curriculum.

Now what do you think you do after primary school? You go to secondary school, right? Primary's the first stage and secondary's the second stage. There is nothing in between. No stage one and a half.

So what do you think my class did after primary school? Naturally we went to Transitional school! No, I'm not making this up. Transitional school really existed, although, apart from my class from St. Mary's Lochee, I never met anyone else who encountered it. It felt to me a bit like going to the bus stop an hour earlier than usual then just waiting there for your bus to come at the normal time. We were to tread educational water: four months of getting ready for secondary school and letting Mrs. Watt's class catch us up! We weren't happy about that aspect, that's for sure.

It was really weird not going straight to secondary school. No-one appeared to have the slightest notion what Transitional school was or how it worked. The questions were stacking up: Who were the teachers? Where was the school? What uniform did I have to wear? Was I a primary or a secondary pupil? What was I going to learn? And most importantly, were the school dinners any good?

Now that last point was uppermost in my mind as I couldn't tell whether I would be near enough to get home on foot at lunchtimes. I had enjoyed Mum's lunches most school days for seven years. I think I'd had to go to school dinners maybe two or three times for various reasons in my time at primary school and I had to admit the food wasn't all that bad. My only hesitation had been when presented with a substance I'd never seen before – pink custard with a skin on top. When first shown this concoction it looked to me like the big plastic jug contained the remains of a wee pet that had been pureed in a blending machine like the one Grandma had in Leeds. The colour suggested a fatal accident. Apart from that, the food in the refectory was ample and edible.

Eventually, just before our final day at St. Mary's Lochee, Mrs. Balbirnie gave us a letter to pass to our parents; a letter she said answered all our questions. Eddie and I set a good pace home that day, anxious for our Mums to reveal our fate to us, but there was in fact no need because Walter opened his letter outside Wullie Fawn's, the barber's. I wouldn't have done that in a million years and neither would Eddie, but Walter as always was a law unto himself and opened it as if he was his own Dad. Despite disapproving, we bent over his diminutive frame to find out what was to happen to us. The letter said we'd be attending St. Joseph's primary school until the summer holidays, but a special bit of the school, one classroom in fact, with just the one teacher. Her name was Mrs. Adams, and we were horrified to read that she was the wife of the Headmaster of Lawside Academy where I was headed in August. I immediately pictured her as a warty old hag with a pointy head and huge hooked nose. This was going to be scary.

None of the three of us knew where St. Joseph's was situated in the town, so we still didn't know how we'd be going to and from school and whether we would have to eat school dinners. Walter had it all worked out already. He would ask his Mum for dinner money but spend it on cigarettes and then sell them at a profit. He reckoned he could easily have his own smokes and his dinner plus a couple of bob in his pocket by this method. Once again, despite knowing that what he planned to do was very wrong and that he would definitely not get into Heaven, I was seriously impressed with his intelligence and flair for business.

It turned out that we had to stick with our St. Mary's uniforms at Transitional school, which was a great relief to lots of families like mine, already saving hard for the secondary uniforms we'd need in August. Mum was able to tell me exactly where St. Joseph's was, and that settled the question about lunch. It would be school dinners from now on. I'd have to take the number 26 bus down Lochee Road then walk down Polepark and up Edward Street to the school. The school itself was on the Hawkhill opposite the Whitehall Theatre. But most of us in the class were consoled by the fact that we'd still be together for four months before having to say cheerio to old pals.

We started our temporary stay at this new school by breaking a significant number of windows. Not deliberately mind you. We had almost immediately instituted a daily challenge football match between our *'Transi'* class and the primary seven class of St. Joseph's, to be held in the big playground to the north of the main building. There then followed a hugely unfortunate run of bad luck whereby over a short period several wayward shots on goal all managed to result in broken windows. That just wasn't fair, especially since the families of the inaccurate strikers had to pay for the repairs. Their Mums and Dads coughed up the cash to the Headmaster but took their displeasure out on their boys in various painful ways, mainly the freezing of pocket money until the sum had been clawed back, probably just before their twenty-first birthdays. Even Mrs. Adams begged us to be more careful, if only to avoid the Head's wrath. She, by the way, turned out to have no warts, no pointy head, no crooked nose and, as far as we could see, no broomstick. She was lovely and a bit like my Auntie Lizzie, especially her smile. So we promised to take greater care with our shooting, especially after an ominous lecture from the Headmaster.

However, the very next lunchtime, when I dashed from my position in goal to thwart an enemy attack, I lashed out at the ball, thumping it back down field as planned, but also sending my right shoe straight through the staffroom window, not as planned. Teachers' faces, all mad with rage at having had a really big fright in mid-sandwich, appeared in the window frame, demanding to know who the culprit was. There wasn't much hesitation before fifty-odd pairs of eyes turned towards me, some in pity and some in accusation. My hand went up and I was gestured inside.

This time I was genuinely scared. After the previous day's warning of dire consequences, I expected no mercy. I anticipated several strokes of the belt (why did we always say "strokes" as if the Headmaster was going to pull the leather strap gently across my palm?), and possibly worse still, a summons for my parents to come up to the school to explain the errors in my upbringing. My legs were shaking as I was called into the Headmaster's study and I was a bit surprised to find Mrs. Adams was already there. She made a slight gesture as if to suggest all was not lost, but in my alarmed state this had quite the opposite effect it was intended to have.

As you'd expect, the Head tore me off a strip for my carelessness, but then to my confusion, he started asking me questions about my brother and my wider family. I didn't understand the reason but I answered as best I could. Then, as soon as he said my mother's family name "Casciani", it dawned on me that he must know one or other of my relations. It turned out to be my uncle Pat Casciani with whom he'd served in the Forces and knew from when Pat had played football for East Fife. The fearsome Head admitted he'd kicked his own boots off many times when playing and he even smiled a bit as he was remembering it. I honestly could not believe my luck. I was saved.

Outside, Mrs. Adams advised me strongly to make sure my laces were extra-tight from then on, as she couldn't promise there'd always be mercy. I never realised how much I loved her, or my uncle Pat.

Although we all had our dinner-money, we didn't always use it for the good, wholesome meal our parents expected us to buy. Not by any stretch of the imagination. Remember that in our opinion we were big boys now, finished with the childish world of primary school and on the threshold of secondary school, pretty much making us adults if the truth be told. So we started buying adult things instead, things like Highland Toffee, Smokey Bacon crisps on a roll, Ski yogurts (particularly the pineapple flavour) and Sports Mixture! Ok, so these didn't exactly constitute most adults' daily diet, but it was the first freedom that many of us had wrenched from our parents, now that we had to take the bus to school and travel a huge two miles from home. This allowed us to pick and choose what went into our mouths at lunchtime, and within this minor revolution, the bread roll with crisps in the playground held sway over beef stew and rice pudding in the dinner-hall.

It was at Transitional school that I was the victim of some verbal bullying by a classmate, a boy called John whom I'd known and played with for several years and with whom I'd never had any problem. That of course made the whole thing all the more hurtful as I could find absolutely no reason why he suddenly started on me. Why hadn't he done it years ago? I just didn't know. But I reckon it would never have started if I'd kept my clothes on.

You see, we were enjoying a warm spring in 1965 and it became a habit for us boys to strip off our shirts and ties during the lunchtime football game. I followed suit, but I also decided to remove the vest Mum insisted I wear to keep the cold out of my chest, especially after that nasty bout of pneumonia I'd suffered a couple of years back. As I pulled the tight vest over my head, John suddenly burst out laughing and screamed to all and sundry that he could see my ribs sticking out of my chest.

He wasn't wrong. In those days there were a lot of kids in Dundee whose diet was pretty poor and who would never be accused of getting fat. I was one of them. Just turned 12, I was still like a stick, but now, as my limbs stretched and stretched, my thin torso was exaggerated and my lack of a tummy left the upper half of my body like a skeleton's chest. I simply hadn't seen this as a matter of any importance until that moment when it was announced to the world that my ribs were so prominent you could play a tune on them like an xylophone!

John called over a friend to come and take a look at "Bones Burton" and that was that. For the next three months or so I had a nickname I came to hate, one that often drove me to the point of tears. I was particularly easy meat for the boy who had first drawn everyone's attention to my physical appearance. Thank you John, you can tell I didn't let it bother me.

And so my class spent four months in an educational Limbo in the care of the magnificent Mrs. Adams. She taught us French, Maths, History and Geography and read with us through H.G. Wells' 'The War of the Worlds', plus some basic Physics and Chemistry. Teaching of Art, Music and P.E. were left to visiting teachers from the secondary schools who all seemed to be strict and unfriendly in comparison. Except for the horrible nickname it was a particularly idyllic period in my schooling that left me feeling like I was being taught on an island out in the ocean somewhere. I'd more or less left primary school behind but the trauma of going up to the big school and being a first year, right at the bottom of the pecking order again, had yet to arrive.

By the time we reached the summer holidays I quite liked pink custard.

2

Collecting

Some of our dinner money didn't get spent on sweets, crisps, drinks or cigarettes. We regularly reserved a small amount to buy bubble-gum cards which were becoming ever more popular amongst us kids. I think maybe we were all slowly but surely losing our innocence, and finding the world around us contained nastiness and cruelty. The people who manufactured these cards were clearly well aware of the tastes of young teenage boys because they had a brilliant knack of catering perfectly for the preoccupation we all suddenly had with blood, gore, pain and death.

My first collections of cards were pretty innocent - *"Flags of the World"* from a bubble-gum series and *"British Birds"* from packets of Brooke Bond Dividend Tea. Both were highly educational and I memorised as much as I could from each series. I kept two albums full of the cards, stuck on the pages with condensed milk, Mum's 'perfectly adequate' replacement for a tube of glue! Sticking the cards into an album meant I needed to have two copies of each card as they all had the photo on the front and the information on the back. This was a truth you learned as soon as you had irrevocably stuck on the first card.

Before long I could say *'Cheerio'* in Polish, knew the capital of Argentina and could tell a sparrow from a robin or a tit. I even knew that female blackbirds were brown. Later, Joe and I were to go hunting for eggs whose colours were described on the cards. We'd prick them at both ends and blow out the contents before nestling them on a bed of cotton wool in a shoebox. It was great fun though we never could compete with cousin Tony's ancient blown Ostrich egg. But before that, having just turned twelve, I needed something more suitable for my age and the cards came along at just the right moment.

One day I noticed one of my classmates flicking through a handful of cards in the playground at St. Joseph's. I went over to have a look, to see if he was checking his collection of the latest cars or maybe up-and-coming football stars. But what I saw had a profound effect on me. He was examining drawings from a series called *"American Civil War"* and they were without doubt the bloodiest and also the most frightening things I had ever seen. Soldiers were being bayoneted as they lay injured, men were running around in flames, others were being trampled beneath the hooves of horses pulling cannons, and corpses lay impaled on sharp wooden stakes. I thought these were brilliant: I had to have them! That very evening, I started my own collection and, to catch up, I went a week or so with only a small bar of chocolate toffee for each lunch, spending the rest on as many cards as I could afford. A bonus came in the form of replica Confederate banknotes which were also in every packet. They were the first foreign 'money' most of us young Dundonians had ever seen.

Before long, our general lust for all things gory was brilliantly catered for with the release of a series on the Second World War called *"Battle"*. Torture and Death were the main features of these cards and their explicit nature was massively prejudiced in terms of how they portrayed German and Japanese soldiers. Political correctness had of course not yet been invented. As a result, any killing by British, American or Allied soldiers was glorified, while the 'dirty' Japs and Jerries were cruelly massacring what seemed to be an unusually big number of people (many being women with surprisingly large breasts). This final detail caught the attention of many of us and added an extra dimension to spending our money on these cards. We were well and truly hooked.

War was also the subject of the third series I started to collect, but this time it was based in the future and took the disturbing form of an invasion from Outer Space. *"Mars Attack!"* had me hiding my head beneath the sheets some nights, worried that a metal umbilical with an eye on the end was about to appear at our bedroom windows and reduce us to ashes with a burst of white-hot rays. The invading Martians, with faces resembling cucumbers with eyes and a mouth, absolutely revelled in using their ray-guns on everything and everyone. They happily set people on fire and reduced cities like Washington to ruins. Despite some nightmares, my friends and I loved all this terrifying chaos.

For quite a while these three card series occupied our young minds day and night, and I think they brought into our lives for the first time the idea that people didn't live forever. In my own case, it wasn't so much the aspect of dying that worried me but more the exposure to excruciating pain that I saw on the faces of the victims on the cards. Tucked up in bed, I'd try to decide whether I'd prefer to have a bayonet through the eye, have my head cut off or be burned to a crisp by a death-ray. The bayonet thing sounded particularly nasty, the head-chopping was awful but pretty quick (though what if you still had your brain working in your severed head for a few minutes after the event?) and the burning up in flames was almost too sore to be imagined. In the end, I plumped for simple beheading, but I needn't have worried as no-one ever considered taking a sword to me.

The subject matters of these cards were the first things I intentionally didn't share with Mum and Dad. Up to that point, I quite openly let them know everything I had done and what I was going to do. To my brother Joe that was ridiculous. But I was a devout young boy tortured by Catholic guilt and over-particular conscience, so I'd found it very difficult to hold back information whether asked of me or not. If I got into trouble at school, I would eventually let them know, even though I knew it would probably cost me a clip on the ear or bed with no tea. Mum believed firmly in docking of pocket money if I misbehaved, leaving me penniless for the whole week. It would have been easy to keep quiet, but I blurted out my guilt time after time. Joe just used to shake his head.

Yet things were at last starting to get a bit different. I had an idea my parents wouldn't have approved of my growing interest in pain, torture and death and I'm absolutely certain Mum would have taken a dim view of me looking at cards containing drawings of women with pointy breasts. So I started to keep such things to myself. It was subtle at first, as simple as not sticking the albums below their noses as they sat watching the TV, but as my guilt started biting, I chose to find little places to store my cards out of sight. On a shelf up high in the haunted wardrobe was one, under Joe's mattress was another (well I wasn't totally stupid, was I?) and underneath the boxed-in bath via the corner access hole was the third and probably the best. That one came into its own later when I had more sensitive material to hide from my parents.

3

Charleston

The nearest shops to 593 South Road were at the foot of Craigowan Road, a short hill a hundred yards from our flat. There was a cooperative store, a post-office, a baker's, a butcher's and a general store. The post office was also the newsagent's where I had my paper round and it was the place where I bought my sweeties and comics. As the bus stop for downtown was directly opposite and the new St. Clements's Church was just fifty yards away, I spent a fair bit of my time down that way, especially after they built a children's play park next to the bus stop. This quickly became the hub for dozens of boys and girls on the estate.

The local shops with the playpark beyond

Football continued to dominate our free time and, although the majority of our games took place in the field next to the Eiffel Tower pylon, the swings in the new play park also doubled as pretty reasonable goals with their uprights and crossbars. There were two sets of swings set about eighty yards apart, the ones nearest the shops for older children and the far away ones with cradle seats for younger ones. In the evenings, once the park attendant had chained up the swings to each side, the play park became a tarmac football pitch, except that it had a roundabout in the middle. Typically of young boys desperate to play out their dreams, we just incorporated into any mazy midfield run a chip of the ball over this obstacle or a swerve around it. And long clearances from defence regularly came flying back at you with interest, depending on the rotation speed of the roundabout and how many kids were on it at the time.

One of my new football pals down at the play park was a tall lad called David. He had very obvious skills, both on the tarmac and in the air, and was one of the players I met over the years with that supernatural ability to jump up and hang there waiting for the ball to arrive at his head. This accounted for the hundreds of goals he headed past me at the swings despite my attempts at resistance. Then, one day, David stayed outside the play park fence and didn't join in the game. When we asked what was wrong he told us there was a chance he'd one day be signing a youth form for Dundee United, one of the two big football clubs in the city, and could no longer play on a hard surface in case he got hurt. He looked really sad that he couldn't join in and he stayed there watching the game rage on. Then he didn't come round any more. Fifteen or so years later I watched full of envy as he scored a famous twenty-five yard "toe-poke" for Scotland against Brazil in the 1982 World Cup in Spain and attained instant sporting immortality. He was of course Davie Narey.

My circle of friends gradually widened a bit more and I began to hear and see attitudes and behaviours I hadn't really witnessed before. It was as if I was coming out of a cocoon made by my family, neighbours and schoolmates. Outside of my restricted environment, not everyone and everything in Dundee was as nice as the world I knew, although most people I met seemed to be pretty normal. There were surprisingly few Crazies about.

However, one weird guy did live right on the corner opposite the post office. His name was Jock Gordon and, with that awful level of cruelty that only children can attain, my friends baited him incessantly. You see, in the thirties and forties Jock had been a boxer in the boxing booths around Dundee, and some said he also had a proper boxing career before that. Unfortunately, constant brutal blows to his head had taken their toll and Jock was what Mum called "punchy" or punch-drunk, with a nasty form of brain damage to which boxers were prone.

This injury gave Jock a strange juddering gait, as if the ground was shaking beneath him as he walked, and the condition made him a prime target for derision from the local children. They'd sneak up and tap him on the back, or knock his bonnet off then run away. They knew he'd try to catch them but realised he would never get anywhere near them as they fled in mock terror. Adults who saw this would jump to Jock's defence and lead him back to the relative safety of his flat. They'd also reprimand the kids for being so nasty, but the culprits had had their fun and just shrugged off the criticism.

I didn't join in this harassment. It just seemed to me that this old man deserved our pity, not our scorn, because we weren't on the planet to visit misery on people less fortunate than ourselves. Having said that, I was guilty too, because I kept running with the pack while these torments were being inflicted, but in my own way I tried to make amends by adding Jock to my "God bless" list when I said my prayers at night. I also took him the odd bag of coal that Joe and I collected from the railway embankment, and that wee gesture made me feel a whole lot better. To be perfectly fair, why Jock cycled around Charleston on a wobbly bike with upside-down racing handlebars I'll never truly understand, given his difficulties with just walking. I can't count the number of times I saw him lying bruised on the road surface with his bike wrapped around him. On one occasion he missed death by fractions when he came off on the S bend at the post office, right in front of our bus. Poor old Jock! I hope he's happy now.

At the top of Craigowan Road just round the corner from our flat there stood a block of four semi-detached council houses that were reserved exclusively for policemen and their families. In the second one down lived the Adair family, including a wee girl called Lisa who was pretty as a picture with ribbons and pigtails. I often used to stop there on my way down to the shops for Mum, get permission to take Lisa with me, and set off with her down the road hand in hand. I was the youngest of my generation in the family and I liked to pretend I had a wee sister to look after. Nobody thought it was strange that Lisa and I were such good friends and no-one ever made a derogatory comment.

I also remember the really old lady who lived in the last close before the shops, only ten yards away. I was well known in the housing scheme and she often called me to her door and asked me to fetch her one or two groceries from the shops. She was a trusting soul and would give me her purse with her pension in it inside her shopping bag. On a fine day she'd sit out at the front of her close in the sunshine and she liked me to sit beside her and listen to stories about the old Dundee. She told me what it was like when she was young and how she'd met Queen Victoria. I didn't mind doing little things for her and some years she'd reward me at Christmas with a selection box.

Joe and I with uncle Jud and our Leeds cousins outside 593 South Road

4

Shops

The next nearest Charleston shops were at the far end of Dunholm Road, which was also the terminus for the 29 bus. Sometimes we stayed on past our stop and went on to the terminus. We always did this if there was a prospect of the bus conductor having a "square go" with some irate passenger who wouldn't pay his fare or had otherwise transgressed. I'll never forgot one time when the passenger and conductor disembarked at the terminus, the bus driver took temporary charge of the conductor's money bag and ticket machine, sleeves were rolled up and a genuine punch-up took place there and then.

The 29 Terminus

This was quite marvellous to watch and drew a fair crowd of spectators. The fisticuffs seemed to be governed by understood rules of engagement and the passenger just backed off when he'd had enough. I never heard of a bus conductor losing a fight and it seemed to me they all knew how to handle themselves. The drivers didn't get involved at all which was a great relief to me as I didn't like the idea of my Dad trading punches with some local gorilla.

The next set of shops was in Craigmount Road near to where my pal Eddie lived. I'd go to these shops quite often because the Camperdown Library was in the middle of the row and I was a bit of a reader just like Joe. But where dear brother was delving deeper and deeper into fantasy and horror with Tolkien and Dennis Wheatley, I was looking for books by Anthony Buckeridge about Jennings and his pal Derbyshire. I'd already read about Tom Brown and Billy Bunter, and the descriptions of life at boarding school were totally fascinating for a wee boy who attended a normal state school. Nothing could have been further from the reality of school life for working class kids in darkest Dundee, but I couldn't get enough of the adventures of these two semi-posh boarders and the pranks they'd play on the schoolmasters.

The carefully censored library and Buckeridge's books in particular were unlikely to damage my boyish innocence, but the grocer's shop to the left offered me my first taste of illicit substances. On the penny tray (in name only by then) next to the flying saucers, liquorice, egg & milk dainties and blackjacks, were two kinds of cinnamon sweetie.

The Craigmount Road library

The Lucky Tatties were already a confirmed favourite of mine but the cinnamon sticks had a different attraction. These long sticks were just okay at best when chewed, but one day I had seen two boys put the sticks to their lips and light the other ends! They were able to smoke the sticks like cigarettes.

I was immediately intrigued. Mum and Dad both smoked plain Woodbine in those days so I was quite used to the idea of smoking, given that they smoked constantly inside our flat just like most other adults. Lizzie and Cissie didn't smoke but I put that down to them being unmarried, assuming there was some kind of connection I didn't fully understand. I think that almost all of my other relations smoked too, aunties, uncles and cousins, and all of their friends.

So I contrived to go to the shops with Eddie and Walter one evening to try to smoke a cinnamon stick. Once we'd bought one, we slunk off behind the shops. As you might expect, Walter produced a box of matches and Eddie and I puffed away on the long spicy root. Walter smoked a real cigarette of course while the other two of us took turns drawing the sweet cinnamon smoke into our mouths. Walter dared us to inhale the smoke, but that led to such a spate of coughing and spluttering that it put me off going that far ever again.

There was also a final set of shops opposite St. Clements's Primary School. My folks' main reason for going to those shops was to buy fish and chips from the chipper at the top of the row. But once I was going to secondary school I often found myself over at the chipper buying stuff from the kiosk near the front door, purely because my first love, Frances McKay, now a pupil at St. John's, got herself a job there. I spent much of the little money I had on rubbish at that kiosk but Frances sometimes slipped me a free penny chew or white mouse. I thought I had a real chance when she gave me a Rhubarb Rock for nothing, but I was so nervous I probably failed to actually say anything to her, and she went off me.

I can't recall how often they bought fish and chips from the chipper for tea, but I'm pretty certain that it wasn't frequent, as Mum and Dad never seemed to have much spare cash, and they were always making their own chips with the "old faithful" chip pan. The fat was always a packet of lard bought from the local butcher and each packet's contents were used many, many times before being replaced once there were too many "bits" in the hardened lard.

The Brownhill Road shops

Dad's chips were known to be as good as anyone's and he put it down to letting the water escape from the cut chips before putting them in the net and lowering them into hot fat. He estimated the temperature of the boiling lard from the whiffs of blue smoke rising from the pan, that being the sign it was time to add the cut potatoes. His other secret was to never try to make too many chips at one time, but to make two batches one after the other, keeping the first batch hot in the gas oven while the second lot fried in the pan. What a genius!

We didn't eat chips every night, but I'd have to admit we had them for tea more often than not, quite frequently with nothing else to accompany them. By the age of thirteen I was expected to take my turn making the chips in time for Mum and Dad coming home from their jobs at around half past five in the evening. Dad had trained me to turn off the gas and throw a damp tea towel over the pan if the contents ever caught fire. Thankfully I never needed to do that.

Right up until I went to Lawside Academy in August of 1965, we'd never had a fridge. Instead, the houses were equipped with a cupboard that had a grille on the outside wall, allowing fresh air to cool the food inside. Mum called this the "cold press" and this is where we kept the butter, milk, eggs and any fresh meat, though as Mum tended to buy that kind of stuff on the day it was to be eaten, there was rarely any fresh meat or fish to store anyway. Cheese was Dairylea segments for Dad and we also kept a piece of rock-hard weeks-old cheddar which Mum would grate over the macaroni on a Thursday, Thursday being Macaroni Day.

In the lobby, between Mum and Dad's room and the living-room, we also had the "hot press" which housed the hot water tank and was therefore where Mum kept the bed linen. Our pyjamas went in there too, so that when we went to our freezing beds they were warm to put on, though never as roasting as when they came out of Auntie Mary's

Baxi in Coupar Angus. The side wall of the hot press protruded about two feet and faced down the length of the lobby, so by hanging a cheap dartboard on it, we had our own Darts Alley. Fierce competitions took place in the winter, and we all played a lot. When we finally came to redecorate the house and re-paper the lobby, we found a surprising amount of damage to the plaster just below the board. It seems that none of us in the family were very good at hitting low targets like Double Three.

Charleston was brilliant in those days. Like other parts of the new Dundee, as well as having interesting shops, it was clean, bright, had great facilities, friendly people and was about as safe as you could ever hope your local area to be. Even at closing time at the Gaiety Bar there was rarely any bother, most of the patrons being happy to give a rendition of their favourite songs or reminisce loudly about the good old days as they made their way home to a choice of *"The Sky at Night"* or *"The Four Just Men"* on TV, before the Epilogue led up to Closedown. Those who nodded off after the odd drink would be awakened by an annoying high-pitched sound which I'm sure was broadcast for that very purpose.

5

Coupar

I spent so much time in Coupar Angus, even as a newborn baby, that it easily qualified as my second home. It was just a few miles from Dundee and was the Casciani family muster point in time of crisis or celebration. Aunts, uncles and cousins galore would spill out of the flat at 44 Princes Croft. Auntie Mary and Uncle Stan managed to accommodate an endless list of guests, thanks to imaginative combinations and arrangements such as rooms filled only with the females or males of the family. As I was the youngest, I was often the exception to the rule and would find myself at bedtime the sole male in an exclusive female world of fluffy slippers, cotton pyjamas and huge, enveloping housecoats, their wearers topped with curlers and headscarves. If I ever had to sleep in the all-male rooms, I found the snoring and breaking of wind annoying, and I was constantly disturbed by the male adults, all of whom would have been at the pub, getting up in procession in the middle of the night to pee.

Auntie Mary had a frying pan the size of Edinburgh. It was black iron with a huge looping handle over it and it was the most important item in her kitchen.

Joe, me and Auntie Lizzie outside 44 Princes Croft

At breakfast time Mary could be found breaking dozens of eggs into it to serve up to whatever starving throng had sheltered beneath her roof the previous night. Meanwhile an endless supply of bacon would be spitting angrily beneath the gas grill, igniting the fat in scary yellow flashes. The two items would of course come together on large white plates that Mary whisked through to the living-room and plonked before her grateful guests. Waiting your turn was absolute agony as the adults were usually served first, followed by the children in descending order of age. Being the youngest had its disadvantages too.

One of the many Christmases in Coupar Angus

I was often sent to fetch Mary's groceries from *'The Buttercup'*, a general store on the town square owned by Ellen Dunn. My aunt would write out a list of things she needed in a notebook with a red cover, put it in her shopping bag and send me away to the shop - with no money. At the other end, Ellen would take the notebook, open it, compile a bundle of groceries, jot some prices and a total in the notebook and then put everything back in the shopping bag. She would then send me off with a word to take care. If it was Friday, I could be sent to the same shop with no list and just Auntie Mary's purse. Ellen would take the purse from me, remove a certain amount of money from it and return it to me for safe keeping. Once or twice she asked me to pass on the message that she'd only taken half the due amount, as there was an awful lot to pay. She knew it would have left Mary with nothing to see her through the rest of the week.

Auntie Mary in The Buttercup

The focal point of the village was the Cross, where the Dundee road came in from the south, crossed the railway line and met the Perth to Forfar road at right angles. This was where we got off the bus to start our visits and also where we took it back home at the end of another fun-and-games weekend with our cousins. Dominating that dropping-off point was Pacitto's café and ice-cream parlour, which was *the* place to sit and chat if you weren't old enough to go into the pubs or indeed if it was mid-afternoon or after ten pm and the hostelries were closed. The highlight of this cafe for me was a hot orange drink, served in a glass with a metal cage and handle to protect your fingers from the boiling liquid. Older teenagers preferred to order the very trendy "coke float" because the scoop of Italian ice-cream dropped into a glass of coca-cola was not only tasty but was also a boost to their with-it image.

It was a fairly quiet wee village but in the early sixties a football legend came out of it. He was one of Dundee's championship winning team of 1961-1962 and later the player who'd be described by Tottenham Hotspur's Jimmy Greaves as "the best player I ever played alongside." This Coupar boy was Alan Gilzean, Scotland's top goal scorer in two seasons, an international star and in many people's opinion the best header of the ball Scotland had ever seen. And I once got a lesson from him on how to head the ball. Amazingly, despite already having a fine sporting reputation, Alan still lived round the corner from Auntie Mary in Strathmore Avenue, opposite the chicken factory. In those less avaricious days football players didn't get a wheelbarrow of cash for every game they played, so most of them lived quite ordinary lives away from the fields of dreams.

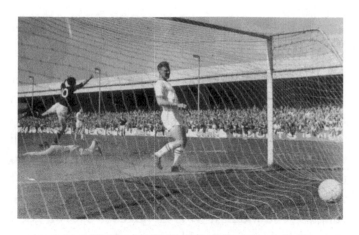

Gilzean scores as Dundee win the League

Right opposite the Gilzean household was a field where I often joined the local kids at the weekend for a friendly kickabout. One Sunday that I would never forget, Alan Gilzean came out of his house, crossed the road and stood at the fence separating the field from the avenue. He watched with interest until one team reached twelve goals (we usually played *six-and-change/twelve-the-winner*) then he called us all over. We eagerly responded to his unexpected invitation and couldn't believe our good luck when he asked if we'd like a few tips to improve our skills. What I remember best is Alan lining us up and throwing the ball to each of us. We had to head it back to him, and he taught us how to time our jump correctly and use our foreheads to knock the ball to him as strongly as possible. At that moment I don't think any of us were aware of just what a privilege it was to get a coaching session from one of the biggest football names of the sixties.

Coupar Angus was also where I learned freshwater bait fishing, a rather more subtle sport than sea fishing. Whereas our weekends down at the docks in Dundee were great fun, they required no skill whatsoever, simply the ability to throw a line into the sea and the strength to pull it back in. The rest was luck, or as was usually the case, lack of it. If we caught a flounder it was a huge stroke of good fortune and a very stupid decision by a hungry fish. Freshwater fishing was a whole different game of tease, entice, trick and trap. Dangling a tasty worm under the nose of a trout was no guarantee of a catch, nor was pulling a shiny, glittering lure past its house, assuming it was at home. My cousin Peter led me through the basics of baiting the hook, fixing float and lead weights, casting and waiting or moving the line through a particular area.

My education in this art culminated one sunny summer's day when I caught my first trout. I was almost always with Joe or Peter or both, but that day I was alone, sitting on a pipe above the middle of the stream that ran to the north of the Coupar Angus railway line. I rolled a piece of bread in my mouth before fixing it as best I could to a small hook, set six inches below a green and yellow float. The bait survived my cast, which often it didn't, and I settled down to what I expected to be another happy but fruitless pursuit of my first trout. Suddenly I was pulled from a daydream by the disappearance of the float and the bend of my rod, and as I raised the tip I could feel the heavy vibration of something on the hook. Forgetting all I had learned, I simply reeled in as fast as I could, trying not to fall off the pipe into the stream in my excitement. Despite my panic there was no 'nearly' this time. The fish gave up fairly easily and hardly struggled to save its scales. Had it tried harder there was a fair chance I'd have done something wrong and it would have escaped, but it didn't. It was a beautiful shiny fish weighing about nine ounces (ok, not Moby Dick but fine by me) and thirty minutes later it had been gutted, beheaded, grilled and eaten. I did the last bit.

I'd love to say it was the first of many fish from the Coupar burn, but it was in fact the first of only five that I caught before someone poured toxic chemicals into the water and killed all the fish. This was a crucial event as it pushed us further afield to the river Isla, the pond at Halliburton and Stormont Loch on the road to Blairgowrie.

The Isla was to prove poor pickings for us dedicated anglers. I think it was because we were all extra-careful about not falling in. It was common lore amongst the kids that the Isla was full of deadly currents which sucked you down and into river-bed holes full of barbed wire and old bicycles.

The river Isla at Coupar Angus

Clarky's Hole was one such spot, the resting place I assumed of one Mister Clark, deceased. As we couldn't afford equipment for fly fishing, we had little chance of snaring one of the salmon that came up the Isla, but one item of special interest to us was the presence of grayling below the bridge on the Blairgowrie Road. The sandy bed was the reason for this rarer fish being there, but though I did see a few, I never caught one.

Halliburton was Peter's favourite place to net a bag of trout. The fish seemed to jump onto his line lemming-style time after time while anyone else was lucky to get a nibble, never mind a fish on the hook.

It was on our way home from this pond, with Peter pedalling his bike while I sat on the seat, that I seriously endangered his marital prospects by letting my foot get caught in the spokes of his rear wheel. The stop was sudden and his pain obvious. He wasn't keen to have me as a passenger after that.

Peter plus guitar of course

Stormont Loch was a different fishing venue altogether, being packed with giant pike and shoals of perch whose dorsal spines kept the predators away. Peter had a close friend whose surname was Hay, so naturally we all called him Grass, and it was this big tough lad who showed me how to hunt pike. Bread and worms did not enter this equation. Grass enticed them with a chunk of stinking herring wrapped round a triple-barbed hook, six to ten feet below a gigantic luminous yellow float, visible at distance. His repeated success with this formula raised it above all other methods and we all adopted the technique.

However, it was the way he killed the fish on the shore that set him apart. Having hooked a three or four pounder, he would land it wriggling and puffing on the grass. I stood at least ten yards away, ultra-cautious lest the pike's innumerable inward-curling teeth should come anywhere near my person. We all believed that a pike, having taken a bite of something, had no way of letting go because of its teeth, so it could only chew and swallow or sever whatever it bit. We had experimented with a smaller freshly caught specimen and the toe of a wellington boot and it was clear that the legend was close to the truth. We shuddered at the thought of our foot inside that boot, so we all treated pike with respect. Except Grass. He'd casually wander over, grab the pike around the gills, hold it up and punch it hard in the face with his massive fist. Dead. A brief shiver and the terrifying beast was inert and our extremities were safe. I still wouldn't go near it though.

Larghan Victory Memorial Park was a great place for us to injure ourselves. Almost every item in Coupar's main play park had the potential to kill you if you abused the facilities as much as we did. The big metal Rocking Horse was regularly rocked until its nose hit the ground in front of it and the mechanism jammed, firing all those mounted on it through the air. No parachutes were provided. The Witch's Hat carousel was spun wildly while we stood on the hand bars above the seats put there for sensible riders. At top speed we'd rock the mechanism inwards towards the centre support, causing it to rebound unpredictably, often throwing us off or worse still knocking us into the middle where it was a challenge to dodge the careering metal bars. Dangerous indeed it was, but also the best fun ever.

Joe and me getting up to monkey business

The park also boasted a Pitch and Putt course where visitors could practise their golf skills with a seven-iron and putter. The nine holes spread out over the far side of the park beside the village cricket pitch, but, as the holes crossed and re-crossed each other's paths, this genteel pastime often became a game of hide-and-seek from wayward drives off the tee. Most especially from cousin Peter, whose great skill with the guitar fret board had not translated to that of the mid-iron. He had the uncanny ability to pitch right at your head from a distance of fifty yards, but couldn't repeat this accuracy when he only had a flag to aim at.

Amongst its other hazards, Larghan boasted the tallest and slippiest chute in Scotland, which resulted in more injuries than all the other items put together. The Paddling-Pool was also frequently tinged with red as unwary foot met broken bottle. Yet we absolutely loved that park and went there every time we visited our Coupar Angus cousins. Sometimes we even came back in one piece.

At the bottom of the Back Toll hill in the north-west corner of the village there was a large field on the opposite side of the road from the Isla River. In this field Joe and I, along with Peter and other local lads, would spend summer and autumn evenings trying to kill rats. When the field had been harvested and haystacks adorned the shorn surface, we'd go down there armed with cricket bats and spades, beat the sides of the often soggy stacks and scare the rats into fleeing their nests. Escape meant running the gauntlet of a dozen or so of us frantically swiping at them as they scurried for safety into the hedges at the side of the road. We really liked this game but the rats didn't!

There were other games played there too. Behind a particularly large haystack, I once saw two local kids with their pants down, entertaining a crowd of children by rubbing themselves against each other. Everybody was excited, pointing at them and laughing at what they were watching. The two performers were the centre of attention but though I joined in the laughter at their antics, I have to admit that I didn't really understand what was going on.

6

Berries

The chance to stick your hand in a wasp's bike, carry a heavy bucket dangling from a piece of string round your waist all day, and plod up and down drills of wet bushes in badly-fitting wellington boots was just so attractive that nearly everyone I knew spent the first three weeks of the summer holidays at the berries. The local countryside for ten to fifteen miles around Dundee was a patchwork of berry fields that burst into life in June and July every year. At ground level the strawberries ripened first, then the tall bushes of raspberries three or four weeks later, giving the Carse of Gowrie an unrivalled reputation for the quality of its fruit. Such remuneration as could be earned for your hard labour provided you with spending money if you were going to be having a holiday, while lots of people without regular employment swarmed to the fields to make as much as they could while they could.

I hated getting up at six o'clock during the school holidays. That just wasn't fair. Motivation however came in the shape of having my own money to spend on whatever I liked, and the opportunity to get up to mischief with my friends. Not to mention my sadistic mother's penchant for putting a wet sponge in my bed if I refused. So, despite my preference for a long lie-in, conformity it was. A rushed breakfast would be followed by a family effort to prepare our 'pieces', various sandwiches designed to see us through the day. Mum's filling of choice came from a strange wee jar with a lid you prised off with a knife and had a thin rubber seal around the lip. This was Shippam's Salmon Spread, a kind of paste with a not entirely convincing taste of the king of fish. I suspect the nearest this stuff had been to a salmon was when the delivery lorry drove over the Tay Bridge. However, I got used to it and the flavour was something I always associated with the fruit harvest.

To wash down our pieces, Mum would prepare a Thermos flask of tea big enough for the entire population of Dundee. It was more like a small dustbin than a flask and couldn't fit into her haversack so it had to be carried separately in an old shopping bag. Not surprisingly, for dessert we ate the berries. They were plentiful and fresh from the husk and above all they were free. If I was in luck, Mum would surprise me with a bag of crisps, knowing that I not only loved eating them but I also loved rummaging inside for that little bag of salt.

With the day's sustenance organised, there was a final check to ensure I had my piece of string or one of Dad's old ties round my waist. This was necessary to support a Luggie, the portable picking bucket which, once full, emptied into a larger pail

These literally provided slim pickings for those of us who were out to earn a lot of cash, but no farmer ever wanted to waste any of his precious crop, so even the few berries hanging on the thin outer bushes had to be harvested.

Auntie Lizzie at the Caddam Road Coupar Angus

On my first visit to a berry field it took me most of a day to completely fill one of the big buckets with raspberries. It must have weighed about seventeen pounds or so, meaning that I was in line for six or seven shillings payment at the weighs. Once full, I took my heavy bucket to the end of the drill, covered the top with leaves, marked it with a stone and went back up the drill to finish picking it clean. When Mum decided it was time to weigh in, we brought the rest of the harvest to the bottom of the drill. I can't describe my shock when I saw that the fruit of my labour was no longer there. The bucket was gone, the berries were gone. As a consolation the thief had left the stone.

I was naturally upset when I got back home, and I spent an unusually quiet evening alone in my room reading or crying. The world was obviously full of dishonest people. I was angry with God for not looking after me, especially since I was still thinking about going to work for him. I decided that an early night was needed, so I was in bed by ten o'clock, and ten minutes later my Beano was on the floor. I closed my eyes.

No-one had prepared me for what came next. It wasn't funny. The first time, it was actually quite alarming. You've worked hard all day in the berry fields, you've picked maybe five thousand berries with your own fingers, you've eaten fifty or so yourself and you've brought some home in a bag. You're tired and you need rest. You close your eyes .... and all you see is berries. Not just one or two, but millions of them, all fully ripened in your subconscious, inescapable. How can you see something even with your eyes closed? That's berries for you. I was even more upset at having to sleep with berries I'd picked and had stolen from me. There they were, mocking me remorselessly, not letting me forget the day's tragedy. The world clearly held no end of cruelty.

Thankfully as the weeks progressed I did manage to get some of my fruit to the weighing-in point, rejoicing in the reward of a handful of coins and the power such riches would bestow on me. At the end of one particular week I was keener than ever for the day's toil to come to an end. As I'd told my brother, I intended to go straight to Woolworth's to buy my first ever camera. Having priced both the camera and the spool of film at an earlier visit, I knew I had enough to launch into the glamorous world of photography. I would even have time to hone my skill with the lens for our upcoming caravan holiday, this time at Kinkell Braes on the edge of St. Andrew's in Fife.

7

Horrors

Despite the weariness from berry-picking, once the cry of "Berry up!" announced the end of picking for the day and we were all taken back home to Charleston in the ramshackle berry-bus, I ran all the way to Lochee High Street and into Woolworth's. I emerged the proud owner of a Kodak Brownie 127 camera pre-loaded with a spool of black-and-white film. I would be the envy of the street. I trotted back home less quickly, not wanting to risk damaging my new possession. Joe was waiting for me outside on the pavement, eager to inspect my purchase, but I'd only let him look at it and not touch.

The iconic camera

We decided to take the first snap over in the field at the Eiffel Tower pylon, as we reckoned that would be a suitably dramatic backdrop for such an iconic moment. We rushed over the embankment where the railway once ran and Joe set himself up in a cool guy pose leaning on the lower girders. I checked that the tiny window in the top of the camera was displaying the figure 1, pointed the lens at my brother and clicked.

We were excited at the success of our first photo-shoot, so we dashed back over the road and up the stairs to tell Mum all about it. The road was safely crossed, we got through the close and we charged up the stairs. On the second-top flight the emotion of the moment must have got the better of my brother and, as he reached the top step, he threw himself into a spontaneous handstand. I was running close behind him, arms stretched out in front of me, both hands clutching my precious new camera. The heel of Joe's leading foot cleanly knocked it from my grasp and sent it spinning towards the stairwell ceiling.

I gasped in horror. I looked up to see my camera arc back down towards me, still spinning and with its neck-cord trailing. I was going to catch it. At that speed, I'd have no problem. I had caught many a tennis ball flashing towards me and they were even smaller than this. How could I miss? But then there was an awful crash and snap of plastic that stopped me in my tracks. I saw the roll of film hit Joe, fall to the floor and bounce down the stairs. I was so shocked that I didn't even cry out. I stared at Joe in disbelief. Why had he done a handstand there of all places and then of all times? He couldn't say anything that would have been appropriate. And worse still he didn't replace my camera for me. He said he couldn't afford it just then.

The Eiffel Tower pylon and our flat behind

Ladies were interesting because they usually thought we were "lovely boys" and often gave us sweets, while men tended to totally ignore us and speak to Dad about football or world events. I know Joe had dreams of some gorgeous girl minus her parents sitting opposite him and inevitably falling madly in love with him, but that never happened either. I just liked sitting between Mum and Dad if I could, because it felt safe. However, I'd have happily sat next to Alan Gilzean, now of Tottenham Hotspur, if he'd been up to see his parents and was on his way back down south. Unfortunately, that never happened either.

A highlight of the journey south for me was when we'd pull in to Newcastle Station. It was a major stop and involved seemingly hundreds of people getting off and on our train and jostling for compartments along the ridiculously narrow corridors on one side of each carriage. The hustle and bustle was exciting but I liked leaving it behind when we pulled out onto the splendid Tyne Bridge, unlike Mum who was of course busy bracing herself for a brief but fatal plunge into the Geordie river.

Each time we reached York, Uncle Jud was sure to be there waiting for us, having bought himself a platform ticket to ensure he could give us a welcome at the earliest opportunity. As soon as Dad stepped off the train, he would stride over to his brother, hand extended and greet him with a very manly *"'Ello, our lad!"* Jud would reply in a similar foreign tongue something on the lines of *"By 'ell, you look grand, our Frank!"* and that was it for the entire duration of our holiday as far as Dad's accent was concerned. As the days passed, his Yorkshire accent would get thicker and thicker until even Mum was struggling to understand what he was saying. Maybe he was affected by the vast number of Yorkshire puddings he ate during the holiday.

On the odd occasion, we wouldn't go straight to Leeds from York Station but would pop down to the King's Arms pub to let the adults have a pint or two (driver included) by the side of the river Ouse. They would also often have a last pint in York on the way home, and many years on, after going down to attend the funeral of Jud's wife, Dad managed to fall backwards into the river while helping Jud reverse the car into a parking space at that pub.

It was January, freezing cold and he was fully dressed, so he nearly drowned. We were in Dundee and got the news from him by telephone, yet we couldn't help but see the funny side of it. Luckily for him he was sober, but it was very, very nearly a tragedy. Joe and I laughed about it for years until we finally visited the spot where he'd fallen in, and only then did we realise how close we'd come to losing our Dad.

Where Dad fell in

Safely arrived at Grandma's house, or sometimes Jud's, Joe and I would rush to meet our cousins Maria, Paul and Maureen and quickly catch up on what had been happening during the previous 12 months. The three of them had about as little knowledge of our lives in Scotland as we had of theirs in Yorkshire and sometimes the conversations would start off with the most basic of questions such as "Do you have electricity?" or "Have you heard of The Beatles?" Though it was 1965, communication between us was limited to rarely more than one call a year from the phone in Mary's house next door, so it was easy to get completely out of touch with events on the other side of the Border.

And so we spent a week or two with our grandparents, uncles, aunts and cousins. Joe and I sometimes didn't know exactly to whom we were talking or to whom every child belonged, but the holiday weeks presented us with an even bigger problem. Because we came from darkest Dundee, they hardly understood a word we said! To be fair, we didn't always pick up what they were saying first time either, as they had fairly thick Yorkshire accents that contorted some ordinary English words as much as we did.

A trip to Bridlington with the Leeds family

They also had different words for everyday things we believed were universal in the English-speaking world. For example, "Mum" was "Mam", an ice-cream cone was a "cornet" and worse still, a "slider" was unknown to them: they only had "wafers". This came home to me at the age of 12 when I was sent out to the ice-cream van and came back almost empty-handed as the lady couldn't understand my order. A similar experience at the chip shop taught me that Yorkshire folk ate fish and chips and not "fish suppers", and I wondered why anyone would want mushy peas to accompany them. As she prepared our orders, the lady in the chip shop asked me if I wanted "scraps" with them and, for the life of me, I couldn't understand why I was being offered little stickers of angels and cherubs to go with our tea.

Another difficulty was of course that they didn't like our money. Scotland used a whole range of its own notes at that time printed by the Bank of Scotland, the Royal Bank of Scotland and the Clydesdale Bank. When we travelled south to Leeds, our parents' pockets contained some of these notes along with Bank of England pound notes Mum had deliberately been hoarding for the previous few weeks. Maybe I was being over-suspicious, but it seemed that every time I was sent to buy something, she gave me a Scottish note, which inevitably meant that *I* was the one to face a fuss being made by some shopkeeper who didn't want to accept the "funny money". I never found out if they actually had the right to refuse our notes: some point-blank refused; some accepted them without question and most accepted after it was clear they'd otherwise lose the sale.

The cause of the fuss

Grandma's house always fascinated me. That's because the living-room and the kitchen (where she appeared to spend the majority of her life making Yorkshire puddings) had an adjoining wall that contained a rather convenient hatch with a sliding door. Thus, Grandma was able to hand through a never-ending stream of cups of tea and biscuits to the assembled company of Burtons, as well as get Grandad's attention in record time if he dared to linger too long in front of the television while she was slaving over a hot teapot. You could tell that he'd have loved to brick up the gap and get a few minutes more peace.

If you sense here that Grandma was a bit of an old battle-axe, you'd be wrong and yet right. She was a typical strong Yorkshire woman and mother.

Grandma Gertrude Burton

Although I never actually saw it happen, Mum told me how her mother-in-law would set Sunday lunch for one o'clock, and on the stroke of one she would set off down the road to the local pub, the Fellmonger. She would stride into the bar and march her sons back up to the house, despite the fact they were all married and in their thirties and forties! Grandma didn't suffer fools gladly, I assure you, but I mostly remember her being very kind to me and asking me lots of questions about my progress at school. And I did very much like her Yorkshire puddings.

Grandma and Grandad with their children

9

Lawside

In Mid-August of 1965 I set off one Monday morning for what I felt was the most important day of my life so far. Mum had got me out of bed extra early and ensured I gave myself a good wash in the bathroom sink, having put the immersion heater on a whole hour before to guarantee there would be hot water in the tank. After an extra-large bowl of Sugar Puffs, a cup of tea and two slices of toast, she helped me with the top button of my starched new white shirt, checked my tie was straight, made sure my hair was combed and my new shoes polished to a dazzle. Then she made a last-minute inspection of the contents of my haversack for pencils, pens, rubbers, rulers, a protractor, a set of compasses and at least two pencil-sharpeners, then pronounced me fit to go to Secondary School.

Yes, with Transitional School behind me, I was off for my very first day at Lawside Academy and boy was I proud! Mum was clearly proud too and shed a wee tear as she gave me a kiss on the forehead and put the school cap Auntie Lizzie had bought for me snugly on my head. It had the Academy crest embroidered on a badge sewn on to it. She handed me my week's dinner money and sent me away with a final "Don't forget to bless yourself!" while

Lawside Academy School badge

gesturing to the font of the Virgin Mary hanging by the front door. I carefully dipped the fingers of my right hand into the holy water, made the sign of the Cross for protection and left the house. I hurried down the stairs, through the close, up the steps to pavement level and raced down Craigowan Road to the bus-stop opposite the shops.

Why didn't I go with brother Joe? Well, although Joe was also a pupil of Lawside Academy and about to start his fourth year of study, he would actually be attending a totally different building from me. He had already been away for a year from my destination, Lawside Annexe, and was currently at the original Convent School on the side of the

75

Dundee Law. Pupils moved from the Annexe to the Convent site after years 1 and 2. Like me, he'd be moving to a brand-new Lawside Academy when it opened in a year's time, but only then would we be together in the same premises. Joe and his pals were destined to be the last pupils to have classes in the Convent School, the one Mum had attended way back in 1928.

So I would never set foot in the Convent as a pupil, because my first year would be spent in the Annexe, just behind St. Joseph's Primary School. As we'd attended Transitional School there, it meant we knew exactly how to get there, where best to get the bus home and which local shops provided good alternatives to school dinners. So I intended to catch the same Number 26 bus that I'd been taking for the previous three months.

Perhaps I should have been suspicious when I noticed rather strange looks from some older boys at the bus-stop, but I put it down to my exceptionally smart appearance. When the bus came, I followed them onboard and as usual made my way upstairs, to my preferred seats on the typical Dundee double-decker. As soon as I reached the top of the stairs, there was a huge roar from the rear seats, and boys and girls started pointing at me and doubling up with laughter. I blushed red with embarrassment and the tears welled up in my eyes, but I didn't know why they were laughing at me. It was only when I saw one of them doff an imaginary cap at me that I realised I was the only kid on the bus wearing a school cap, Academy crest and all! In a flash I whipped the cap from my head and stuffed it into my blazer while the laughter rolled on. One sympathetic woman chipped in with "Leave the laddie alone, he looks very smart". I had no choice but to fling myself into a free seat at the very front and stare straight ahead for the entire journey, until I hurried downstairs on Lochee Road, set off down Polepark and started up Edward Street.

On the way, I met up with some of my old pals from Primary School and I suppose I was actually glad the cap incident had happened on the bus with people I didn't know very well as opposed to my future school mates. They would undoubtedly have tortured me for years about it. In a way it was a close escape and that night I winced as I imagined myself running into the playground with the cap on, grinning with boyish happiness and excitement, only to be greeted by the whole of the Annexe, teachers included, laughing their heads off at me!

When the bell rang, we were all gradually lined up in the playground according to the classes we'd been allocated and then marched off to our new registration rooms. I was placed in 1A Boys, the top-ranked class for boys in first year. So, for the first time, I was going to be taught in a boys-only environment, something I was quite pleased about to begin with. When our new teacher left the class for a moment after checking for absentees, our immediate conversation topic was the very fierce-looking man we had passed halfway up the stairs. He must have had an office off to the right, because he roared out a boy's name as we passed and a second-year lad had to turn and walk past him into a dark, narrow entrance, a look of terror on his face.

Once the timetables had been filled in so that we knew which classes we had, the bell rang again and we were released into a rabbit warren of unfamiliar corridors and staircases. Amidst a sea of bodies, panic was only a breath away as we novices frantically tried to find our next class. Some boys seemed keen to send us all in the wrong direction, but fortunately, a cooperative second-year showed someone the real route to take. Confusion continued until about a fortnight into our time on Blackness Road, when we'd all learned how to get where we needed to be. Some kids took longer than others and some paid the price for late arrival. Teachers didn't offer us much help: we were expected to learn, and learn fast. A well-honed sense of direction would be paramount.

The scary man on the stairs was discovered to be the Annexe Headmaster and we all resolved immediately to avoid him at all costs. I knew that the previous winter he'd given my brother six of the belt for the unspeakable crime of throwing a snowball after the Assembly bell had rung. What's more, he had carried out the punishment in front of the second year girls' class, to ensure Joe would be humiliated if he was seen to flinch or cry. There seemed to be quite a lot of angry folk like him in schools, and few people realised how many demobbed servicemen had just been shoehorned into education jobs after the War. They might know nothing of teaching, but they certainly knew about Discipline. To be fair though, that first day went quite well. I met a whole load of new friends and half a dozen new teachers, and I liked this old building I was to attend for the next ten months. "Playtime" was replaced in our vocabulary by "interval" and the school dinners passed the taste test reasonably well. We entered our final lesson of the day still buzzing with the excitement of the new school and the new phase in our lives. And then things went horribly wrong.

The last lesson was Physics and we were very quickly issued with jotters by a small thin man with a strange accent that I guessed might be Polish. We were to write the notes he dictated as he walked around the classroom. I remember his opening words so clearly: "Matter is something that cannot be created or destroyed...." Now I had been taught to write very neatly so I had to try hard to keep up with his monologue. About three sentences in, he happened to pass my desk, stopped, looked over my shoulder and quietly told me to go out to the front of the class. I almost wet my pants! As I stood there quaking, I couldn't work out what was going on. Had I done something really well or really badly? Had I used a pen instead of a pencil? Was it the wrong jotter?

Sauntering casually back to his desk, the teacher put his hand under his black gown at shoulder level and slowly withdrew a thick leather belt. "This is my Educator" he told the other boys, none of whom appeared to be breathing. He ordered me to put my hands out (which I did of course without question) and proceeded to wallop me on one hand and then on the other, before sending me back to my seat, still without an explanation. I did my best to show it didn't hurt, but my hands were tingling like a severe case of pins and needles and my fingers stung as I took up my pencil again. The teacher came back over to my seat, pointed at my notes and told me to rub them out and start again, this time correctly on the very top line!

Now all through Primary School, my teachers had encouraged us to start a new page halfway along the second line from the top. I was simply doing exactly what I'd been taught, but had fallen foul of a master with a different view who felt no need to explain in advance what he expected of his new pupils. I wasn't the only one who got the belt that day. Although I felt a great sense of injustice, I learned that I'd have to keep my wits about me at all times when the teachers were around, even the two nuns, one of whom was the English teacher and the other, our Latin teacher. There was no question of letting our guard down, even during the prayers in which they led us at the start of their lessons: Sister Mary Bernadette's rosary beads hung from her waist .... next to her belt!

Within the first couple of weeks at the Blackness Annexe, many of us had already started to shun the delights of school dinners in favour of whatever the local shops had to offer. Some of the shops depended entirely on the custom of the school kids to make their business profitable and they never did well during any of the seasonal school holidays. One such establishment stood a couple of hundred yards up Blackness Road in a narrow street called Annfield Row. This shop had set itself up to supply hungry teenage stomachs with exactly the sort of things they craved: pies, sausage rolls, bridies (plain or onion), filled rolls, cakes and biscuits. Its freezer also contained our favourite ice lolly, the strawberry Mivvi. You bit through the bright red ice exterior to expose the gorgeous ice-cream underneath, an absolutely irresistible combination. Sadly, I usually didn't have that extra couple of pennies to afford a Mivvi so it was normally a plain ice lolly for me.

However, what made that shop unforgettable wasn't the vast array of local snacks on offer but its totally delicious soup. We mostly opted for lentil soup although the Scotch Broth was pretty fantastic as well. To cope with a multitude of requests for a cup of his soup every midday, the shopkeeper had been forced to use his initiative to keep up with the demand. This didn't involve investment in a super-big tureen. No, he cleverly saved money by making the soup in a top-loading washing machine! The agitator was kept running to ensure that the vegetables and lentils didn't settle on the bottom. We loved that soup and had no problem with it being served from a washing-machine. The school dinners further down Blackness Road simply couldn't compete.

10

Music

I'd tried to learn a musical instrument at St. Mary's Lochee and I did make a bit of progress, culminating in being able to scrape out *"Au Clair de la Lune"* on viola. But the process of getting to that stage had proven just too excruciating for me to want to take it any further. The practice sessions took place in a classroom other than our own, which was a good thing, and in the company of two or three other aspiring musicians, which wasn't. The instructress was a portly lady with a big moon face and those spectacles with funny wings on the frame that always made the wearers look like owls. My own Auntie Cissie wore them at some stage, and she looked like an owl for sure.

When I say the learning was just too painful, I mean that literally, because the patent method for getting student instrumentalists to play the right notes on the viola was to show us where to press our fingers on the fretless arm and then ask us to repeat these notes ad nauseum. Every time I played a wrong note, I received a sharp whack with a wooden ruler just above my bare knee because I wore short trousers.

That hurt so it did, but it must have motivated me not to repeat these wrong notes because the accuracy of my recitals did improve. After each lesson I would firmly resolve not to go back, but Mum insisted I stick with it and become a musician.

Me in shorts, plus Leeds cousins Maureen and Maria

Though long trousers had now replaced my shorts, instrumental tuition followed an approach to education which had stood for over 60 years. We'd be shown how to do something, asked to repeat what we had seen or heard or read, and be given hours of examples to puzzle over. If we got too many wrong or failed to grasp a concept quickly enough, then we were hit on the hands with the belt (often more than once) and told to go back to our seats and try harder. If we showed a lack of ability we were told we were dumb clucks. We were also belted for talking in class, for getting less than half marks at spelling tests, for being late for school (no excuses accepted) and for forgetting our homework. Other crimes punishable by belting were having no gym kit, saying prayers incorrectly and failing to 'grass' on fellow pupils.

The most surprising thing about it all is that most of us really liked being at school with all our friends. We considered most of our teachers to be fairly decent people, even when they belted us. Our mums and dads had survived this kind of an environment and they expected us to do the same - shut up and get on with the lessons. There was little or no refusal to conform amongst us: rebellion hadn't yet entered our minds. Oh, it did eventually surface but that was in the future. First year of secondary school at Lawside Annexe was neither the time nor the place.

When I finally got rid of the viola about 1965, there was only one instrument I wanted to learn and that was the guitar. Players of this instrument had taken the world by storm over the previous eight to ten years and, with the arrival of the Beatles and the Rolling Stones (but also with the brilliant instrumentals of The Shadows' Hank Marvin), everyone of my age wanted to be a great guitarist. In my family, there were already guitar-playing vocalists, including my rising star of a cousin Peter in Coupar Angus and teddy-boy cousin Tony Brown. Tony had been the first person I heard playing live, bashing out songs by Lonnie Donegan, Elvis Presley and Joe Brown in the bedroom of Auntie Katie's Blackshades prefab. But Peter took it a lot further and started performing in public with his own group in the pubs and hotels: soon the girls were lining up to meet him after a gig and that made a serious impression on boys of my age.

It was through my love for the guitar that I made my first new friends at Lawside, Dougie and Phillip. The former turned out to be a decent player and matured quickly as an instrumentalist, at one point even making his own electric guitar. Phillip actually didn't play but was friends with Dougie and soon we three were inseparable, spending evenings together in each other's houses learning new songs and talking all things Top Twenty. The hit parade was the focus of much discussion among my schoolmates now that we were twelve or thirteen. We all had different opinions on whom we liked or didn't like and who was the best guitarist, singer or drummer of them all. We could listen to our heroes perform either on mono record-player turntables or on transistor radios, which had become the most-requested Christmas presents of our age. But I had neither, so going to a pal's house was a better option than inviting them to come to mine.

My brother Joe then acquired a transistor radio and suddenly we discovered the fascination of Radio Luxembourg. Thanks to this pop music station and its amazing DJs, Joe and I were kept supplied with all of our favourite tunes, or at least snippets thereof. I say snippets because, in an effort to squeeze in as many records as possible on a sponsored show, they'd normally only play the first couple of minutes of each tune. Add to that the annoyance of the station fading away momentarily (usually at my favourite bit of a song) before gradually returning, then hearing all of the best stuff was a bit of a lottery. I liked the funny 'gong' sound that would chime every so often before a voice would tell us "This is Radio Luxembourg: your Station of the Stars".

The transistor radio definitely changed our sleep patterns as well. Our normal routine was bed around ten o'clock or half past, a few minutes reading of either a school book or hopefully something a bit more exciting like *"Roy of the Rovers"* or *"Commando"*, then lights out and off to sleep. There was no other reason to stay awake: the TV closed down at the back of eleven for the night and Mum and Dad would usually be asleep by then. But "Wonderful 208" kept playing pop music until about two o'clock in the morning. That was a huge attraction for us, especially between eleven and midnight on Sundays when Britain's Top Twenty tracks were played. I think the first time I heard that programme, the Rolling Stones were at no.1 with *"(I can't get no) Satisfaction"* which we loved for its wickedness. However, Ken Dodd's *"Tears"* was also a hugely popular song at that time, or at least it was popular with Mums and

Dads because teenagers were far too cool to like that kind of music.

So, on many a Monday morning in my first year at Lawside, Mum had to drag me out of bed to get ready for a hard day's work at school, the previous night's music still playing in my cotton wool head. Thursday was of course the evening we most eagerly anticipated because that's when BBC's "Top of the Pops" was on, giving us all the opportunity to actually see and hear our idols even though they were miming most of the time. We would watch it together as a family, because our parents were still in their 40s, so they were still fairly open to new sounds, although Tom Jones and Kathy Kirby were high up on their list of preferences. "Top of the Pops" would inspire my brother and me to rush off to our bedroom, to see if we could recreate any of the stuff we'd just heard. Slowly but surely, on the old bashed guitar we had inherited from Tony Brown, we began to pick up the patterns of Rhythm & Blues and, given that we were both pretty good vocalists, we started to perform some of the material to a reasonable standard.

By 1965 "Top of the Pops" had become the most popular music programme on TV but it wasn't the only one. BBC's Saturday series "Juke Box Jury" hosted by David Jacobs gave us the chance to hear new records being judged by 4 panellists, some of whom were pop stars themselves. Once each, the

Rolling Stones and the Beatles made up the entire panel. I particularly liked when a new song was voted a 'Miss' and David Jacobs pressed a rude sounding hooter, but that was nothing compared to my glee if the rejected performer appeared from behind a screen as a "surprise" guest. I don't know who felt more embarrassed, the singer or the panellists!

ITV of course had their own pop music programmes such as "Thank your Lucky Stars", where, in a section copied from "Juke Box Jury" teenagers voted on new releases. I remember when a young girl called Janice Nicholls with a broad Brummie accent coined her catch-phrase "I'll buy it and I'll give it 5!" as she awarded the maximum score to a particular song. A second ITV music show "Ready, Steady, Go!" was a bit anarchic for its time with wobbly cameras in crowded studios and a general sense of chaos, but it was a sign of changes to come in popular culture that Joe and I savoured.

Now and again we'd get the chance to hear one of Peter's groups play live somewhere near Coupar Angus. We loved the fact that this meant electric guitars and microphones as opposed to our own acoustic efforts. Soon we had both set our hearts on acquiring an electric guitar, but we'd have to wait a long time. When my new friend Dougie put together his own home-made electric guitar, including pick-ups and long-neck fret board, I was

The Phantoms with Peter on the right

insanely jealous and seized every opportunity to try
it out when we were together. It played so much
more easily than the old acoustic guitar and the
throaty roar that came from his speaker was
absolutely heaven to my teenage ears.

Had we had a piano in the house then I'm sure Joe
and I would have picked that up too. Auntie Mary
had one in her living-room, one that her Polish
husband Stan would play from time to time. Auntie
Mary could play too, as could daughters Renée and
Wee Mary, and at least one of them could get a
tune out of an accordion, so there's no doubt that
there was a strong musical heritage in the Casciani
side of the family. Peter was the only one who
really took his talent outside the family home,

joining a band and trying to become famous. He was in fact very good, at one point playing with the Raith Showband in Kirkcaldy more than once a week and also becoming a member of one of Dundee's most successful bands "Mafia". But, just like thousands of other would-be pop stars of that time, the more mundane pressures of life intervened in his musical story.

Auntie Mary, son Peter and best pal Fordie

The classes we had at Lawside were in a more traditional vein and included learning the science and language of music. We also had to learn 'Sol-Fa' pieces off by heart then perform them out on the classroom floor. We hated doing that sort of music lesson, but much of what we learned that year was to prove hugely useful to us all when it came to trying to create our own tunes. However, in our own time we only ever tried to apply them to rock and roll.

I was still a member of the St. Clements' Church choir and sang every Sunday at eleven o'clock mass. I had stuck this out because the organist and choirmaster was my ex-P7 Primary School teacher, the one and only Margaret Balbirnie. She was such a lovely person and such a brilliant teacher that I found it difficult to quit the choir even when my voice started to break. I particularly loved the Latin hymns we would sing such as "Ave Maria" but it was the section at the end of the "Sanctus" that I loved the best, a three-part harmony that sounded like it was being sung by angels themselves. I can assure you that, by that age, it wasn't angels doing the singing!

My Mum sang a bit, but her songs were usually ballads by Jim Reeves or Doris Day, and she rarely finished any of them because she usually started sobbing. I don't think she was unhappy. I just think she was a bit too sentimental by nature and couldn't stop the tears welling up. "*I Love You Because*" was her favourite, yet she only ever heard it on radio or TV by chance, as she never owned a record player to listen to at her leisure.

Dad had one music-related claim to fame as far as I was concerned. Unlike most of his brothers and sisters in Yorkshire he didn't play any instruments, and it certainly wasn't his ability to sing *"On Ilkley Moor Baht 'at!"* whether drunk or sober. Nor was it the accomplished performances he thought he could give on the spoons or the comb and paper. No, it was the fact that in October 1963 he had seen that band called the Beatles getting out of a car on Shore Terrace to enter the Caird Hall via the back door, trying to avoid being mobbed by their fans. It never crossed his mind that by 1965 the band he saw arriving in Dundee would be global stars.

11

Games

'*Kissie-Catchie*' was a game with a single purpose: to give everyone a chance to learn how to kiss. The boys chased the girls, caught them and kissed them. Then the girls chased the boys, caught them and kissed them. This was an early example of equal opportunities. But it didn't always quite work out like that, because we weren't all at the front of the queue when God gave out the good looks. So some of us didn't get caught, and consequently kissed, even if we stood still and waited. When I say "some of us" I mean me of course. I thought I was at least cute, if not dashingly handsome, and my dear Mum kept reinforcing that I was "the bonniest of them all". Add to that the fact my auntie Lizzie would always tell me that my smile would break lots of hearts one day. Clearly that day hadn't yet arrived and I had to trot around pretending to be running away but watching Ian, the local heartthrob, being pursued by every girl in the street. They even queued up to kiss him. Not fair.

Even at twelve years old, I still sometimes played this game, and I did get some action when it was the boys' turn to do the chasing. The problem was that time after time the girls seemed to find a quite extraordinary turn of foot to escape my clutches and although I was a faster runner than Ian, he managed to catch all of them with apparent ease. So I spent a lot of this game kissing two particular girls who weren't all that fast and who had clearly been in the same place as me in the good looks queue. On the odd occasion when I did get my hands on Marilyn or one of the other more popular girls, just as I made to kiss her she'd turn her face to the side and only let me kiss her on the cheek. I duly obliged as she hadn't actually refused to kiss me, had she? And maybe her lips were sore because she did an awful lot of kissing.

If we didn't feel like running after each other, we played an alternative game 'Truth, Dare, Double-dare, Promise, Kiss, Command'. No chasing was required. You simply picked a forfeit and generally ended up kissing someone, no matter what you chose. How economical. There may have been the odd obligation to do something silly like slap yourself in the face, but mostly it was kissing until people got bored with it. After all there was only so long you could kiss a girl, wasn't there? And then what? I certainly didn't know for sure, but I had a strong feeling there was a direct link to closer relationships.

To take the romantic theme further, there was also a way to see under a girl's skirt. It was to play 'Farmer, Farmer, May I Cross the River?' To be successful in this game you had to be wearing something in the colour the Farmer decided would allow you to cross an imaginary river. If he said "Only if you have on.....blue!" then you had to show you were wearing something blue to stay in the game. Obviously. But we boys had worked out that, when it was your turn to be the Farmer, if you asked for a colour not on their outer clothing, then the girls would be forced to show you something hidden. This was a "win-win" situation for us. All we had to do was choose a typical pants colour like navy blue or white, and a girl might well raise her skirt to prove she was wearing the requisite colour to stay in the game. We thought we were really crafty and we never considered that the girls might be quite aware of what we were doing. Just into our teens, not all of us completely understood why it was so naughty for a girl to show off her pants: we'd just been told it was.

Trees, fences, stairs and washing green poles all had one thing in common: they all provided a safe haven when playing 'High Tig'. Technically so did standing on a brick or hanging from a window-sill, but these forms of escape weren't used as frequently as the others. My first-year pals and I still loved this chasing game, where you were immune to capture as long as your feet were off the ground. Except maybe for the Sahara Desert, the game could be played just about anywhere, including indoors if you wanted to. I was really fond of its simplicity, so I remember getting very annoyed at the "modern" rule someone introduced, a rule that turned out to be hundreds of years old.

In Dundee we called it "putting your chaps up", which was a raised thumbs gesture that granted short-term immunity from capture. This changed the dynamic of the game completely because the chased person could now stay in the game even when cornered. I did use it myself at times, but always felt it spoiled the game. My instinct for fair play suffered a blow once this rule came in. I quickly tired of hunting down my friends with energy and cunning, only to be denied victory by this inexplicably stupid rule. It must have been invented by someone who couldn't run very fast or couldn't climb. I soon gave up playing.

Another evening in my first year at Secondary school, from our living room window, I saw two drunk men in the field opposite us, playing a game of *'High Tig'* with a number of policemen. To make sure that they were safe from capture, the two men chose to climb the Eiffel Tower pylon, but for some reason when the police came closer, they kept on climbing higher and higher. I had never seen anyone go beyond the barbed wire which snaked right round the whole structure about fifteen feet off the ground but these two drunks wriggled through that defence and continued upwards. To my delight and Mum's horror they quickly reached a point just short of where the electricity cables passed through the pylon.

Disaster seemed inevitable. I couldn't make my mind up if I'd prefer them to fall or get frazzled by the fifty-thousand volts as both forms of exit would be equally dramatic. Then it occurred to me that the frazzle would be better because a fall would inevitably follow electrocution, and that way I'd see both.

The Eiffel Tower Pylon

Mum found it so terrifying she just couldn't take her eyes off it. She expected the policemen to go up and help the two men descend. However, Dundee's Finest didn't look too keen to move into rescue mode, so they contented themselves with shouting advice to the less-than-sober human flies. I hoped that if there weren't going to be any fatalities then at least the police would get one of those great big sheets for the men to jump into, like I'd seen on television. So it was a bit of an anti-climax when the two men finally agreed to climb back down and then did so unerringly like two seasoned steeplejacks. Mum was delighted when they reached the safety of the ground. They were promptly marched away by the bunch of burly cops but I was a bit disappointed that the drama had ended so quietly.

The pylon incident was rather a damp squib to be honest. Unlike the rocket that flew right through our bedroom window that year on the Fifth of November. That particular squib wasn't damp at all. In fact it was quite the opposite; intensely hot going by the way it set fire to my curtains, burned loads of the wallpaper and left a big hole in the cover of Joe's bed. I wasn't in my room at the time our surprise visitor burst in, but we all heard the window pane smash and rushed through to see what had happened. Mum was worried it might be a burglar (we were 2 floors off the ground remember!), but the reality was even more alarming. I have to say my Dad was very masterful on this occasion, unhooking the wire holding up the curtains, then grabbing my pyjama bottoms (I wasn't wearing them at the time) and beating out the flames.

What was even more interesting than the fire was the discussion between Mum and Dad which followed. Mum pointed out that, although the set of curtains was destroyed beyond repair, as was the cover on the bed, the sheets and pillows appeared to be unscathed. I could scarcely believe my eyes as she lit up a Woodbine cigarette then held the lit match to Joe's bed, allowing it to gently scorch the pillow. She did the same with both his sheets, removing them once some obvious damage had been done. I just could not understand this and thought she'd lost her mind. Things were clarified two days later when the Insurance Inspector came to the house and assured Mum that she was covered for the loss of the curtains, all of the bedclothes and enough wallpaper to redecorate the whole room. For once I had the sense to keep my mouth shut! Thanks to that misguided missile our room was soon as good as new. But I did wonder whether Mum would enjoy explaining all that to the priest the next time she knelt down at Confession.

12

Blackness

Joe was at times a big help with settling down at Blackness Annexe: well, he was my only brother after all and had spent his first two years of secondary school there. The dilemma was always whether or not to believe the details he'd give me about the teachers and subjects, as it quickly became clear that some of his advice was not entirely accurate. What's more, he often had two versions of the information he shared, one for when Mum and Dad were around and one for when he was alone with me. Needless to say, away from adult ears in our bedroom, he would tell me some pretty scary stuff about how awful the teachers were, how disgusting the dinners were and how difficult all the schoolwork was going to be. Sometimes he was right.

I had arrived at Lawside Annexe fully aware that this was going to be a much greater challenge than my Primary School had been. I had achieved high standards in those early years, partly because Mum made me work so hard at my studies at home, ensuring I did all my homework to the best of my ability then making me revise my lessons of that day. I'd been either first or second in the class from Primary 2 until Primary 7 and only Elissa, John, Linda or Maureen had ever challenged me seriously in that achievement. If they got close, I just worked harder. I was also kept on my toes by the general expectations of my family, who'd seen Joe Casciani set the bar high with his University Degree, travel abroad and studies at the Sorbonne.

The Burtons at Tony Brown's wedding

But Joe Casciani (a cousin but old enough to be my uncle) wasn't the only academic success in the family. My own brother Joe was doing very well three years ahead of me and had a good reputation for his facility with words, winning prizes and getting articles in the School Magazine and so on. Cousin Wee Mary was also very bright at school, in fact she was considered a model pupil at Lawside Convent until she dyed her hair platinum blond at fifteen, sending the nuns into paroxysms of horror. When told to change it back or leave the school, she left! My other cousins were all doing very well either in education or employment, and Tony and Jimmy Brown were now both in the RAF.

Tony Brown in uniform

Cousins Jimmy Brown and Renée Grayson

Despite all of this, I was apprehensive that the work was going to be overwhelming in first year and I might not cope, never mind might not have any time to relax and have fun. So I applied myself very seriously to my studies from the first day and determined to live up to the family standards. Admittedly some of the work was quite taxing and there was certainly plenty of it. We had so much Maths, Physics and Chemistry homework that it could take me the whole evening to complete, and we seemed to have some kind of test on a daily basis. We even had to work hard in Religious Instruction, learning the words to prayers (English and Latin), hymns and Bible stories and parables.

It therefore came as a great relief to discover that I was up there with the best of them when results came out: indeed I was sometimes the top scorer in French vocabulary tests or in Arithmetic - or, to my utter surprise, Latin. But I was only ever likely to be a runner-up overall in the year group. As fate would have it, in 1A Girls was a young lass of phenomenal intellect whose knowledge seemed at times to be boundless. Her name was Jennifer Adams and she was the daughter of the Lawside Headmaster and of the lady teacher who'd taught us in Transitional School.

Jennifer was uncatchable. If I got 98% for Latin, she got 100%. If I got 96% for French, she got 99%. Now as you might expect she wasn't the most popular girl in First Year, but had anyone paid any attention, they'd have found her to be a pleasant, kind person who just happened to be very, very clever. She had no airs or graces, she was sociable and she smiled a lot. No doubt her family background ensured that she had to put in as many hours of study as me, but, where I was allowed to be less-than-perfect, there was extra pressure on Jennifer never to falter, and she didn't intend to disappoint her parents. We did however share one important thing. We were never invited to join the class in-crowd. This was to prove important in later school years, but for the moment I was too busy working to notice the little cliques that were developing.

The teachers started off by calling me Joseph a bit too often for my liking, having taught my dear brother earlier, but I was referred to as "Burton" fairly universally. There was no insult intended or taken from this. We were mainly called by our surnames, as were the girls, even by the cooler teachers whom we tended to find more affable. One of these was Mr. Campbell, a very popular and likeable teacher (we secretly called him Pete but never to his face) and he taught us French in that first year, although he appeared to be part of the Classics Department. Pete Campbell was a refreshing change from the array of serious, unsmiling faces that stood in front of us each day. I thought they were all a bit grim, but they were probably just doing that teacher thing of pretending to be much worse than they actually were.

Being taught some subjects by nuns was a bit unusual. Given my formative years in a conventional Catholic family and my time as an altar-boy, I still had the idea that I might have a go at being a priest. I guess it was perfectly natural in those circumstances and no doubt Mum and all her sisters were continually offering up candles and novenas to ensure that I embraced the vocation. Nuns therefore weren't alien to my Catholic heritage, being right up there with priests (well, nearly.) I'd been taught they were worthy of respect and veneration as "special" women. But having them as teachers was a different story.

Sister Mary Monica could have been a saint herself. Not only did she exude an aura of enlightenment and peace, but she was also the nicest of all our teachers, a kind, loving woman who only wanted the best for her pupils. She never seemed to get upset (even when we boys had a particularly flatulent lesson) and I can't remember her not having a smile on her face. She was petite, pretty and so, so gentle to everyone in the class, even those who clearly didn't deserve it. She taught us English in a room near the top of the building and we all loved her. As often happens with the nicest of people, she died not long after we left her care, but by then she'd made a huge impression on me and my classmates.

Her colleague Sister Mary Bernadette most certainly didn't fit the above description. She was strict, tough and aggressive, with a booming voice that made us tremble. Her belt hung from her waist alongside her black rosary beads, announcing that tough love would be applied when necessary, and she applied it on a daily basis. She started every lesson with prayers but made us extend our right arms parallel to the floor before sweeping our right hands to our foreheads as she bellowed "In the name of the Father ...." She would search among us as we stood reciting the Lord's Prayer and the Hail Mary for anyone not joining in with the correct words. This was clearly her foolproof method of spotting heathens with the minimum of effort.

We had our first grounding in Latin from her, conjugating verbs and declining nouns endlessly, not realising that she was providing us with the fundamentals of all the languages we were ever likely to try to learn. At twelve and thirteen, we couldn't see the good she was doing for us but that's just how it was then. We were the kids and she was a teacher and a nun. There was no more to be said.

Most of my teachers were much as I had expected: they were quite nice but had a job to do, not by any means an easy job with 30-odd boys in a room. They realised that I constituted no threat to their authority and saw that they could, thanks to my hard work, announce in the staff room that 'their' pupil had some of the highest marks in the year. I got used to moving from room to room every hour or so, a big change from spending whole years in the one classroom at primary school, and by the Christmas holidays, my friends and I felt like we'd been at the Blackness Road Annexe forever. But then in the run-up to Christmas, the snow came!

Yes, the snow came. Enough to cause disruption to bus services and provide us with the material required for building snowmen and making snowballs. The snowfall made it quite problematic getting to school some days but it was expected that we should make every effort to reach the building, even if it meant not arriving until lunchtime. I often had to walk to school that winter, mainly because the buses had to negotiate a steep hill on Craigard Road just after the stop where I got on, which often proved just too much for their spinning wheels and crash gearboxes. I once saw one slide helplessly back down that hill, slipping from one side of the road to the other and taking a parked Ford Anglia with it, both vehicles coming to rest halfway down on the corner of Ravenscraig Road.

The route I had to walk to school, usually on my own, wasn't particularly easy as it involved climbing steeply up Elmwood Road from Lochee West Station, then cutting through Lochee Park where there'd be tons of unblemished snow to play in. Then it was over to Blackness Road via Balgay Park, and finally downhill with plenty of pavement slides all the way to the Annexe. With a heavy haversack full of school equipment, I'd be wrapped in my duffel-coat passed down from a neighbour, my face protected by one of mum's scratchy hand-knitted balaclavas. My wellington boots kept the snow out but devastated my skinny legs as the tops rubbed against me at every step, despite the long trousers I now wore in secondary school. The alternative was no better: my school shoes had holes in them and were lined with cardboard and polythene bags to stop my feet from getting wet. Joe's shoes were no different.

By the time I'd covered the two miles to school and despite the knitted gloves I was wearing, my hands would be absolutely frozen and I was desperate to get inside and put them on the pipe radiators in the classrooms. The teachers would warn me that I'd get chilblains but, as I had no idea what chilblains were, I kept my hands on the hot metal, enjoying the heat penetrating my skin. I never did get chilblains, or if I did, I never knew that's what I'd got!

The snow completely disrupted our schooling, with teachers and pupils alike turning up at all sorts of times of the day, leaving half-classes with or without someone to give lessons. Where no teacher was available, we'd be sent to the school library to sign out the book of our choice. Then we were expected to go back to class and read in silence for as long as it took for normality to return, a normality we sometimes hoped might never come back. At interval and lunchtime, outside in the playground, there would be a scene of utter chaos, but it was brilliant fun with snowballs arriving from all angles, long slides the length of the courtyard, unfortunate victims being 'Bero-ed' and girls screaming as we forced handfuls of snow down their necks.

One day we were all lined up outside the refectory standing in snow as it gradually turned to slush, waiting to be allowed in for our school lunch. There must have been fifty or sixty of us, all twelve and thirteen-year old boys, all typically ravenous after a morning's work and all slowly becoming more and more bad-tempered as sleet fell down on us and added to the discomfort we were already feeling. Suddenly there came a powerful forward push from the rear of the drenched queue, which squeezed us all up tightly against the hall door. The crush got more intense and raised voices could be heard from some very angry boys, when suddenly the door of the hall gave a sharp crack as the old hinges buckled under the pressure being exerted on them. Some boys tried to push back against the throng but it was to no avail, as the old wooden door crashed inwards and the front boys went with it.

There was pandemonium as the teachers on dinner duty rushed over to intercept the surge of kids spilling through the hole where the door had been. The unfortunate boys from the front of the queue stumbled to their feet, and were pulled away by the teachers and lined up to the side. I think it was less for their own safety and more to ensure that there was someone to blame. A dozen or so others were added to their number, apparently at random, before the whole lot were marched away for a mass belting event, while the real miscreants from the back of the queue enjoyed a hearty, hot meal. Most of the victims were entirely innocent but nobody dared protest as they left the hall, while inside at table the more fortunate boys tucked in to their dinners with big grins on their faces.

One of the boys grinning that day would have been David Sinclair or "Sinky" as we called him. Right from the outset at the Annexe, Sinky was a bit different from the rest of us. Oh he was clever enough, that was for sure, but what made him stand out from the year group was his street-wise, confrontational attitude to authority. He quickly assumed the mantle of Naughtiest Boy in First Year and, in the teachers' eyes, a real troublemaker. Sinky must have been belted every day of his school career and often more than once a day, such was his love of facing up to people who wanted to rein him in.

Though he was a bit of a bully, we of course thought Sinky was wonderfully daring and he made us laugh at the teacher's expense on many occasions. One of his favourite tricks was to come into our Registration room beside the entrance walkway along the front playground, answer "Here" when his name was called out by the teacher, then quickly slip out one of the huge sliding windows onto the path. He'd then run back into the building via the main door and reappear in the classroom, apologising for his late arrival. The teacher would send him to his seat and open the register to amend the entry for Sinclair. It was hilarious to see their puzzlement when they tried to understand how they'd managed to mark Sinky present just a few moments earlier.

Inevitably on snowy days, some pupils would get hurt and windows would be broken, nothing could be more certain. On occasions, this led to the ultimate collective punishment of us not being allowed outside at interval. This sanction would be announced from a note sent round the classes by the feared Annexe Headmaster, mere minutes before the anticipated bell would ring, and it had the desired effect. It broke our hearts and even raised the odd voice in protest, but inside we would have to stay. We wouldn't be able to get out between lessons either, as the Annexe was self-contained in one big building, so we had to wait for that day's school to end before indulging in the next round of snowy mayhem. Fortunately, unlike in my morning trek, there were plenty of my friends from Charleston to walk home with. Of course having to go through two big parks to reach our area meant that it was often well past teatime when we'd finally present ourselves in Eskimo form to our parents.

Those nights, just before going to sleep, I would say an extra prayer for more snow.

13

Conflict

At the 1956 Melbourne Olympic Games, young Dick McTaggart had risen to fame by winning the gold medal in lightweight boxing, and the people of Dundee were rightly proud of the wonderful achievement of their famous son. Boxing became very popular again in the years following McTaggart's win and clubs like the Camperdown Boxing Club and the St. Francis Club were never short of members.

Maybe that's why, on Christmas Day of 1964, Joe and I each woke up to find a pair of red boxing gloves on the bed. In less than half an hour my nose was bleeding. This painful experience was to be re-enacted repeatedly over the next two or three years despite my best efforts to avoid it. I probably landed the odd punch on Joe myself but that generally only made matters significantly worse as he reciprocated with interest. I spent a lot of time on the floor curled up in a ball, grateful that big brother always respected the house rule of "no hitting when the opponent is down." I was naturally often reluctant to get back up on my feet, as that meant a further barrage of jabs to the face and stomach, the almost inevitable right-hander to the jaw and the collapse down to the floor.

This wasn't fun for me. Even Joe tired of knocking me around the living-room with impunity, and I took little pleasure in running round and round the settee trying to get away from him. Stand and fight? Not for me I'm afraid. The bit I least enjoyed was the white flash. That always happened if I was caught with a surprise punch to the eye or nose, making me turn my head away in case more was following. Now Joe wasn't always in a sympathetic frame of mind when he had the gloves on, so a second swipe quite often *did* follow the first, frequently aimed at one of my ears. Then the impact would come again, followed by a second or two of partial deafness. Oh what a joy boxing was!

So much for my parents planning a thoughtful Christmas present. Thank you Santa, or more accurately, Dad. I'm sure that Mum would never have imagined boxing gloves as the ideal gift to celebrate the birth of the Lord. Clearly it was down to Dad, with some old-fashioned notion that we could have hours of harmless fun trying to maim each other. There would also be the added bonus of ensuring that neither of his sons turned into a Jessie, but each would learn to fight like a Man. It didn't work like that for me. It was obvious to me that if a bigger, stronger person starts to swing punches at you with the intention of damaging your good looks, it's far more sensible to run away and not fight another day. I was no masochist and no idiot. Pain hurt.

Why didn't Dad jump in more often to save me from clobberings by Joe? He'd normally only call time on a bout after I started to cry or bleed. He must have been hoping that, sooner or later, I'd stand tall and give as good as I got. But that never happened. Yet I never really blamed my brother for what went on. He was only doing what older and stronger brothers are meant to do. No doubt it was his duty to beat me to a pulp time after time. I guess it wasn't his fault that I absolutely refused to comply with the Marquis of Queensberry approach to self-defence. Having said that, a little less power in the uppercuts would have been appreciated as would a bit more sympathy and less laughter as I lay on the linoleum.

So taking part in warfare wasn't for me, despite my interest in comics and cigarette cards dealing with the subject. Even though we all loved watching ITV's wrestling on a Saturday afternoon, desperate to see the first challenger to defeat that monstrous 'baddie' Mick McManus, I didn't really fancy participating in the sport. Joe of course took on a fraternal teaching role by showing me how to do a Japanese Stranglehold or a Boston Crab, applying the said moves while I groaned in agony at the effects of a hold well-administered.

I shied away from *any* activity outdoors that involved getting punched in the face. I'd taken a couple of bare-knuckle right hooks at Primary School, so at least I knew what a punch felt like. I had to admit it wasn't particularly pleasant even though they'd left me with no more than a bruise to my cheek. I also found that I disliked almost as much seeing other lads being battered in playground squabbles. It seemed that some boys really enjoyed hitting other kids, but not me: I hated it and hardly ever raised a hand in anger even when I had reason to.

One day, when my pals and I were chasing away some interlopers from our den in the field, I found myself on the dismantled railway track holding a boy smaller than me by the scruff of the neck. I really had no intention of carrying out any of the violence I was threatening, but he didn't know this and decided that if he was going to be beaten to a pulp he might as well get his retaliation in first. He unexpectedly bashed me full force on the nose, causing me to let go of him, and he was off in a flash!

I realised from such events that I might as well stay away from violent situations, as I just didn't have it in me to dish it out. I don't quite know how I was so lucky, but aggression towards me was so infrequent in the whole of my teenage years that I must have had to raise my hands less than half a dozen times in total, and always in self-defence.

This was despite the fact that the mid-Sixties saw the rise of teenage gang culture in Dundee, but my friends and I didn't have anything to do with that.

None of us were violent by nature, although we of course pushed each other around and grappled with each other in "toy" fights, just like any other kids. We simply couldn't see what pleasure the gang members got from kicking a person unconscious or breaking somebody's nose with a head-butt. I guess it's possible that these boys found something in the gang that they'd been missing in their lives, whereas the rest of us had no great dissatisfactions to work off. In Dundee the majority of us youngsters just wanted to get on with growing up, enjoy ourselves and do as little harm as possible.

To us, those gang boys were mindless thugs making themselves feel important by preying on innocent kids. Their wanton violence wasn't just the fun they pretended it was: it damaged many a victim and left a lot of scars. It's a fact that for a while, each of the gangs *ruled* its own turf, but that was only a short-lived thing and thank God it evaporated as the demands of adult life came along. Anyway, why did the Lochee Fleet choose to hate people from Fintry? We just didn't get it. However, when I visited my pal Phillip's house in that housing scheme, I was very careful not to let anyone know that I came from the alien state of Charleston! Most of my crowd steered clear of all this madness and hoped to keep all our teeth.

So we certainly didn't unite into gangs, but we did get together in teams to play various sports, the most important of which was naturally football.

Whilst boxing gloves made me anxious, goalkeeper's gloves made my eyes light up. Just the once, I'd played a game in the right-back position for my Primary School team, one frosty December morning at Camperdown Park. I remember we lost (by quite a lot) and I certainly remember how the hard Mitre football brought me close to tears as the opposition winger crashed it against my crotch from point-blank range. I still wince at the thought! There and then ended my aspirations to play as a defender, so, from that point on, when I wasn't up front trying to head in the goals, I doubled up as the goalie. To my surprise I discovered that I really enjoyed throwing myself around, especially if the ground wasn't too hard.

Most boys of my age wanted to play up front as a winger or centre-forward, the positions from which most goals were scored. However, despite my love of nodding the ball past the keeper, I found I got just as much satisfaction in the goal, stopping a fierce drive or diving to foil a forward. My ideal game over in the field in front of our house was to play as a forward for the first half in a *'six-and-change / twelve-the-winner'* match then play in goal for the second half and hopefully keep the opposition at bay.

Oddly, given my abhorrence of violence, I wasn't worried by the sometimes robust physical contact of football. It was an integral part of the game. I wouldn't hesitate to dive at onrushing forwards' feet or jump to stick my head in where other heads were doing likewise. Sports where the aim was simply to knock out your opponent held no appeal at all for me, but football finally started to toughen me up.

14

Affliction

The worst present my Mum ever gave me was haemorrhoids. At least I assume it was a genetic inheritance from her because she definitely had them well before me. The only other source of this most derided of afflictions could have been the low radiators in the classrooms at primary school, you know, the ones the teacher was always telling you not to sit on because you'd get piles. Well I used to sit on them, especially on a winter's day or after swimming lessons. Linda Gow sat on them a lot too but I don't know if she ever had piles.

Mum wasn't minded in any way to explain to me exactly what haemorrhoids were, neither their precise location nor their negative influence on life. The only obvious symptom of her ailment was a tendency to break wind loudly at inopportune moments, followed by embarrassed apologies to all present. She always blamed this on having piles.

I did notice that when Mum broke wind, either at home or in public, there was never a bad smell to accompany it. Now when Dad occasionally let one go we'd all groan and have to breathe through our jerseys, which we immediately pulled up over our noses. At school, however, my friends and I thought farting was hilarious and we'd compete with each other to summon up the loudest and smelliest emission, especially in confined areas to achieve maximum effect. Our classroom was the preferred arena. The Lochee swimming pool was also favoured, because you always had the bonus of the bubbles rising to the surface before liberating the smell into the air above.

Soon after I was born, Mum had a stroke, brought on by a tiny fragment of my placenta which worked its way through her body until it reached her brain. While she was in hospital recovering, I was farmed out to Auntie Lizzie who reputedly weaned me on macaroni and grated cheese. To be fair, Lizzie was always my favourite aunt and I always had a bit of a taste for the short cut pasta. Mum's stroke left her with a slight weakness down the left side of her body which was only ever apparent when she was eating. If a small piece of food settled on her chin just below and to the left of her bottom lip, she was never aware of its unwanted presence, but Dad, Joe and I would always catch her eye and tap on our chins as unobtrusively as possible in such an event. Mum appreciated that.

I suppose it was natural after four lost babies, two full-term successful pregnancies and a stroke, but Mum was always absolutely petrified of hospitals. She would do anything other than have to go to A & E or attend out-patients or even have an X-Ray. This fear extended to visiting people in hospitals as well and on more than one occasion she had to

122

excuse herself and get help from the staff when she would come over "all queer" in the ward if we were visiting a sick relative, neighbour or acquaintance. The sight of blood had the same effect on her, causing her dizziness if she had to deal with any serious boyhood injuries. It's just as well Dad was usually on hand to stem the flow and patch us up.

My own particular affliction was hay-fever. I began to suffer from this soon after we moved to South Road and I suppose that hours and hours rolling around in the grass in the field opposite our flat may have had quite a lot to do with its onset. I was a martyr to fits of sneezing, incredibly itchy eyes and a distinct wheeze in my throat and chest all summer long, but it was quite impossible for me to stay away from the field where all my pals were playing football, so I just had to put up with it. To soothe my tortured eyes when I finally came back indoors, Mum would give me a wee blue, plastic eyebath containing Optrex, which I had to seal onto my eye socket. Then I had to tip my head back whilst keeping my eye open. It was tricky at first and we wasted a lot of liquid trying to get it right, but once I had the hang of it, the eyebath became my saviour at the end of an evening's play on the grass.

I also had frequent bouts of tonsillitis that caused me to miss the odd day's schooling. I never caught the cold: it was always tonsillitis and it was always treated with Tyrozets, orange-flavoured tablets with an analgesic content, leaving my throat numb but at least less painful. The doctor had me down twice on the waiting list for a tonsillectomy but somehow the operation day never arrived and I gradually grew out of that complaint from about the age of thirteen.

Dad pre-falsers!

Dad's affliction was obvious for anyone to see. In his middle years he sported the worst set of teeth on the planet. To describe them in detail would be invidious, so let's just say they were very, very in need of attention. To be fair, Dad had always said that he would go to the dentist and have them *all* extracted as soon as any one of them gave him a moment of pain. That's exactly what he did, bravely going to Dundee's Dental Hospital and returning the same day a bit bloodied and a touch swollen around the mouth, but otherwise still the same old Dad, making terrible puns about gums and so on. He brought his extracted stumps home in a tissue to show us, but I declined to take a look. Dad later told us how he'd always feared the dentist's chair as a result of some traumatic experiences as a kid down in Leeds. I knew how he felt. I was always pretty anxious before the arrival of the school dentist for the routine check-ups on my class.

My own memories of dental treatment include the horror of a rubber mask being forced over my nose and mouth, causing me to breathe in the gas that would put me to sleep. At times it would take a couple of dental assistants to pin me down and let the gas do its work. Or, worse still, there was the drill whirring and grinding feverishly on my back molars with little or no anaesthesia. I always seemed to bleed a lot after treatment, so I needed a white handkerchief over my mouth held in place by a scarf to keep the cold air out. Whether that was the recommended procedure I still don't know, but lots of children my age could be seen walking around with the telltale scarf over the mouth.

Joe and I did once attempt to recreate the DIY version of dental extraction as illustrated by the cartoon character "Oor Wullie" in the *Sunday Post*. Anytime Wullie had toothache, he would tie a string round the offending fang and the other end to the doorknob then slam the door shut, thereby yanking the tooth rapidly and painlessly from its socket. At least that was the theory. I foolishly wanted to try it when I had a loose tooth. For a start tying a string around a tooth was not an easy job and it required a strong thread, but even after we got the thread in place, it kept slipping off the top of the tooth when yanked, causing me yet further pain and still no relief. We eventually abandoned Wullie's patent method and tried Joe's alternative approach: a well-aimed right hook from a boxing-gloved hand. That did the trick.

Dad had a permanent smile after he had all his teeth out. But this wasn't just because he was ecstatic with the results. It was caused by his new false teeth altering the shape of his jaw and mouth, giving him the appearance of a very happy man, even when he wasn't. He used to liken himself to "Mr. Ed", a talking horse on an American television comedy show. The thing was, I could see the resemblance as well. However, because he was no longer reluctant to open his mouth, Dad really did smile a lot more after his extractions and delivery of his first dentures. It was only a few years later that I helped him get another new set of teeth, when I accidentally flushed his old ones down the loo after he'd been sick with food poisoning. Oops, sorry Dad.

15

Crematorium

Just after the Christmas holidays of 1965-66, we were reminded that we'd soon be moving to the brand-new Lawside Academy, north of the Kingsway. It wasn't an area of town with which I was familiar at all, though I knew it was on the other side of the Crematorium from Auntie Katie's prefab in Blackshades. Neither had I ever been to the Crematorium itself as, coming from a Catholic family, all my departed relations and friends tended to be buried in one of Dundee's cemeteries, especially the Balgay cemetery known locally as 'The Hilly'. Grandma was in there already, alongside Wee Frankie, the brother I had never known. He was Mum's first live child after two still births but the wee soul only managed six weeks of life before succumbing to the deadly Whooping Cough.

It was obviously very exciting to be going to a new Lawside building with all the modern facilities it would no doubt have, and we interrogated the teachers at every opportunity about what we'd have there. As young teenagers, our priorities were first a sports hall, second a swimming pool, third good playing fields and fourth shops nearby. We were rather apathetic about the cutting-edge educational facilities that we were told would be in our new school, although a modern music department and a language laboratory did kindle a small amount of interest from me. Some of my friends talked a lot about what the new science labs would be like, anticipating laser beams, rockets and explosions galore, but at this stage I was struggling with Physics and Chemistry, so I had little interest in that sort of thing. Well, maybe the explosions.

Yes, it had a Language Laboratory

My time at the Annexe was soon over and frankly not much had happened there that could be termed earth-shattering. However, during my time at Blackness it was an entirely different story in the wider U.K. and a lot was going on that would shape the country for years to come. With great encouragement from Mum, the driving force behind much of the success Joe and I were enjoying, I'd started to watch the STV news at tea-time. This was to broaden my horizons as I listened in to reports from all over the world on events with far-reaching consequences.

The criminal world was fascinating what with Ronnie Biggs escaping from Wandsworth Prison and the Kray and Richardson brothers shooting up London, but I was totally horrified as the dark details emerged of the Moors Murders. The murderous Brady and Hindley became household names, and many people were outraged that, before they came to trial, the government abolished the death penalty. Further afield, things were falling apart in Rhodesia as a piece of the old Empire growled for its freedom. There seemed to be death and disaster at every turn, and this began to make me reassess my ideas of the kind of world I was going to be living in.

It wasn't all gloom and doom however, not by a long way. Johnny Hackett just couldn't stop talking about the latest collectible toy car from Corgi, none other than James Bond's Aston Martin, straight from the film *"Goldfinger"*. And yet at the same time as we were enjoying these playthings, we were also intrigued by a new magazine that had begun to appear on the shelves. It was called *"Mayfair"* and the covers hinted at wicked pleasures within. Before long we had all thumbed our way through an illicit copy, though actually going into a shop and buying one was quite simply beyond our courage at that age.

Naughty thoughts and notions were further increased by images of Swinging London in the media, including Mary Quant's brilliant concept, the mini-skirt. It did little to fill in the main gaps which still existed in my ideas of what life was all about, but I became very interested in the amount of leg that fashionable girls were soon baring. Getting a glimpse of 'what lay beneath' became a popular pursuit among the members of 1A Boys and the open plan of the new Lawside's staircases was soon to be of considerable help to us in achieving that.

"Helpful" stairs

One thing I had to give up on just before we moved was the idea of seeing the Beatles play live on stage. After many hit singles, three top albums and two major movies, they suddenly decided to stop touring and concentrate on recording in studios. So they wouldn't be playing for our school dance.

As the May holiday approached, the teachers at the Annexe had us help with packing up the equipment and other things that would be making the transfer to the new building. The furniture wasn't included on this list as it appeared we'd all be sitting on new chairs and leaning on new desks. Clearly no expense was going to be spared. In this way our work wound down fairly quickly at Blackness Road. We always seemed to be doing something other than the scheduled lessons in the last few weeks before the move. Before we knew it, we'd gone and I don't think I ever set foot in that building again.

There was of course a total change in the logistics of getting to the new building on School Road. For a start there was no direct bus link between Charleston and the school. All the buses that headed north, left from Albert Square in the very centre of Dundee. That meant I had to take my normal No.26 bus all the way into town, then catch the 1A or 1B back out towards the school.

That's how we ended up travelling, and we could buy just one ticket for the double journey. On the

No.26 we would all buy a Penny Transfer and receive a small grey ticket from the conductor, to present on the 1A once we changed in Albert Square. The 1A conductor was supposed to use a little gadget to punch a hole in the ticket, but if he forgot to punch it, we could keep it for use another day. That was great when it occurred although it was just costing us one penny to go to school and one penny to get home. Nevertheless, once we were settled in at the new school, we would often save the penny by walking all the way back home via the Timex Brae and the Kingsway.

An alternative for *getting* to school was to catch the number 13 at the foot of the Timex Brae. This bus was the nearest thing to a cross-city link and could drop us at the Kingsway roundabout just down from the Crematorium. Now and then, especially in winter when the buses could be disrupted, we'd end up walking the full two miles from South Road. There were also special buses allocated to take the hundreds of pupils into town at the end of the school day. Sometimes Dad and his conductor would be one of the crews and with a bit of luck I'd get a free trip into town. But the main attraction here was the absolute mayhem when the bell rang for the end of lessons and a huge numbers of pupils would race to board their bus, despite the frantic efforts of the conductors to retain a semblance of order. The crush was incredible, like leaving Dens Park with 40,000 other fans at the end of a Dundee game, but we all loved

133

the pushing and shoving that went on every day at four o'clock.

The inner quadrangle

Our first day at School Road was a huge success. It was warm and sunny, which showed the bright modern buildings to their best with their floor-to-ceiling glass windows and the design, with its central quadrangle, made me feel like we were somewhere special and even slightly privileged. We made lap after lap of the inner courtyard. There was a covered link between St. Andrew's House block and the Staffroom. Just in front of this link was something extravagant and unusual that we hadn't expected to find in any school on earth, never mind our own, something so out of the ordinary that it was an object of fascination for many of us. It was a lily-pond!

Yes, the powers-that-be had obviously decided that their new school would feature decorative areas as well as purely functional ones, maybe theorising that such culture would intellectually inspire the students to new heights of academic achievement.

The Lily-Pond surrounded by benches

Perhaps it might have, but this was Dundee in the Sixties. Before long there was a tradition of accidentally knocking kids into the three-foot deep pond, often as they made their way to the Technical and Art Departments adjoining the gym.

On that first morning the whole school gathered in the assembly hall to hear Mr. Adams welcome us to the brave, new world of the Academy. We were told we were in one of the most modern and sophisticated schools in Scotland, equipped better than any of its rivals and worthy of the most complete respect by its pupils. Vandalism was to be a crime punishable, so it seemed, by death or at least one hundred of the belt! No graffiti anywhere, neither in the rooms, in the toilets nor on the desks. The walls of the classrooms were all painted in bright colours and we were warned to be very careful not to scratch them as we went by with our bags and haversacks.

We were particularly impressed with the amount of outside space we now had. With the seniors having been allocated special areas inside the building for common rooms and prefect rooms, a huge playground outside the English Department accommodated the rest of us with relative ease, allowing us to set up many different pitches for various forms of football. The bike sheds at the bottom of course became the domain of the cigarette smokers, who would duck and dive around the bicycles to avoid being seen. I'm sure they could actually be seen but, especially on rainy days, no-one in authority was very keen to venture out and round them up.

The girls quickly took to walking those laps around the inner quadrangle, linked arm-in-arm, sometimes four abreast, chatting away about the things girls chat about at that age. It was in such circumstances that, two years later, I was to walk past the object of my romantic desires about fifty times one lunchtime, she with friends clockwise and I with my pals anti-clockwise, until I finally plucked up the courage to ask her for a date.

The facilities at the new school met with our approval. The swimming pool was brilliant, the gymnasium large and well-equipped and the playing-fields, a short walk away beside the Kingsway, were extensive and covered in the most beautiful soft grass, or at least they were at the beginning. The classrooms were light and airy, the science labs well-stocked with high tables, stools and all the equipment you could ever need, the dining-room clean, shiny and with room for hundreds of us (although we still had to queue to get in) and there was even a neat little tuck-shop at the back of the P.E. Department.

Mr. Adams and his team had decided that the school would be divided into 3 Houses: St. Paul's, St. Peter's and St. Andrew's. That was pretty much what you could expect at a Catholic senior secondary school: it was saints' names as standard, with not even a nod in the direction of modernity. I was placed in St. Paul's House, possibly randomly, and therefore had to register in the Maths Department which for reasons unknown was linked with that House. These divisions were of little consequence to us except when it came to inter-House competitions, when fierce rivalry would temporarily flare.

Unable to go home at lunchtimes, we all tended to eat school dinners, which were perfectly reasonable unless, being a junior, you found yourself at a table ruled by a despotic senior. Such types were generally unfair in the way they distributed the meals. Food came in trays of 6 portions but younger pupils often had to make do with a small spoonful of meat, vegetables or pudding while those in charge of the table had their own plates overflowing. This evidence that power corrupts left me hungry on more than one occasion and at times prompted me to head for the local shops instead of the refectory.

So there I was in May 1966 admitted to the new one-campus Lawside Academy, at school for the first time since Primary 1 with my brother Joe, although how often he would admit to being my brother (or even speak to me for that matter) would depend largely on his level of moodiness as he prepared to turn sixteen years of age. At least he'd travel to school with me in the mornings, getting on the same buses but preferring to sit with his own band of friends.

Joe entertained me with a couple of stories about how the pupils had celebrated liberation from Lawside Convent School. I thought it was hilarious how someone had removed the capital "C" from the poster showing the famous fruit-growing area around Dundee, the Carse of Gowrie, and how his entire year-group had been 'grilled' military fashion to try to extract a confession from the guilty party, but without success. He also revealed that a daring pal had left lots of taps running in an unsuccessful attempt to flood the premises, but had been intercepted by the notorious "Piggy" Paterson who used his Lochgelly tawse to devastating effect. It never occurred to me that the teachers called their belts *'Lochgellys'* because they were all made in the Fife town of that name.

The one thing no-one had counted on, not even Joe, was the implication of being educated in the shadow of Dundee's Crematorium. The sight of the daily smoke and the disturbing smell of the incinerator doing its work were a constant reminder to us that none of us were immortal, even if we all felt that we were just that.

16

Rankings

Hardly had we settled down to the new premises and to our new teachers than we were plunged into a whole swathe of tests designed to give a rank order for the year group, and setting the boys against the girls for the first time. I knew from the winter exams down at the Annexe that I was ranked well within 1A Boys but we'd heard scary stories about a whole group of super-brains in 1A Girls, including the unbeatable Jennifer Adams. Nonetheless I set out to win the boys' crown if I could and to push those troublesome girls to their limits. They were going to have to be at their best to beat Georgie Burton!

Because we had no mixed classes at that point, it was difficult to assess if the rumours about their enormous brains were true and mixing with them in the playground only helped establish whether we fancied them or not. I got a bit of help from my friend and rival Elissa Soave with whom I'd grappled for supremacy all through Primary School and who seemed to be among the top pupils in 1A Girls. She admitted that neither of us was ever likely to score higher than Jennifer but that we had a chance of being in the top ten if we really went for it. John Duncan was keeping his standards high as well and there were several new girls from other

Dundee primary schools whom Elissa knew were very bright and always answering out in class.

Joe chipped in with some observations on how things were marked by the teachers. Arithmetic and Mathematics were areas where full marks were possible while English was a subject in which the essay-style answer made really high grades unlikely. Science gave you a chance to score high marks, as did Latin and French, but getting 90% or more in History and Geography was uncommon. My previous test results suggested I could get 100% for Arithmetic and maybe even Maths but I had no real pointer as to the other subjects. I'd have to wait to see if I could maintain my record of a prize every year of my schooling.

There was a point to doing well apart from the personal glory. In the system that existed then, how we did in exams was the basis for crucial decisions about our futures, just as the tests had permanently affected me and my friends at the end of primary school. So on a bad day it would be quite possible to come last and end up slipping down the pecking order, ultimately into 1B1 Boys, where some of my pals were doing Technical to my Latin. In 1B1 Girls some of them were learning Domestic Science while Elissa's class had the higher status of taking Latin.

Coming last was also possible if you had a bad memory. Perhaps with the exception of English, everything was tested by asking for learned facts about a subject. For those kids who found it difficult to retain information even in the short-term, sitting those types of tests was a major hurdle. History concentrated mainly on dates and we'd done a lot of work on the Russian Revolution, while Geography was predominantly concerned with places, capitals and industries. Latin and French were all about vocabulary and grammar, with translations from and into English so you had to have a great memory for all the words. Dictionaries were neither available nor allowed. It was just as well that I had a trick memory and my brain soaked up facts like a sponge.

We were also given grades for P.E., Art, Music and R.E. Our performances in sports weren't assessed scientifically, Music was based on knowledge of how music worked with notes, keys and staves, and Art was just your basic ability at drawing. As soon as we had to draw anything that wasn't a horse's head I was struggling. However, we all looked forward to Art because it was taught on the other side of the lily pond next to the Technical Department and that meant we had a couple of minutes outside when moving from the previous class. Sometimes nobody at all would end up in the lily pond.

As a rule, in 1A Boys we were fairly conscientious when it came to preparing for exams. Admittedly some of us put in more hours than others, usually depending on how strict our parents were, but the ethos was one of hard work for success and most of us gave it our best shot. On occasions, I'd pop round to Dougie Mullen's house in Dunholm Road so that we could study together. We actually did help each other with questions on a given topic, although naturally the temptation to get out the guitars and learn a new song was always going to be a winner. We just couldn't resist it. It also slowly emerged that we had different ways of swotting up subjects. I preferred to read something over half-a-dozen times then get someone (usually Mum) to ask me questions. I also found it helpful to rewrite my notes to embed the information in my brain. I didn't have to reflect much on things at that time because naturally none of the questions ever asked us kids for our opinion.

Sometime in late May, the exams took place and there were lots of papers to sit as we moved from subject to subject. Everyone battled through them, scribbling away in absolute silence right up until the bell rang and 'pens down!' We were never allowed to talk until we were clear of the exam room but slowly the noise would build up in the corridor then outside as classmates bemoaned the difficulty of each paper. It was an unwritten rule that you never said the exam had been easy in case you upset someone who might have found it tough, or even worse, in case you turned out to have failed.

For me that year, English, Physics and Chemistry were a bit difficult whereas Arithmetic, Maths, Latin and French were more manageable than I'd expected. The other subjects were pretty average. I discovered to my delight that what I'd been learning in the Latin class was proving really helpful with guessing some of the new words in the French Interpretation and Translation papers. So maybe it did have some use beyond religious matters.

When the results came out I was pleased: I'd been placed third overall in the year group. Needless to say, Jennifer Adams came first, beating us all by a mile and scoring an average of over 90% for all subjects. Second was a smiling red-haired girl with great big glasses: I didn't know her and I think her name was Docherty. Then came me, third, followed closely in fourth place by my old classmate Elissa Soave. Well done Elissa. Mum would definitely want me to marry her now if I didn't join the clergy. It seemed to me she'd been mentioning the forthcoming wedding since Primary 4.

Elissa, Jennifer and me among the prize-winners

This all meant of course that I'd achieved my aim of coming top boy in first year at Lawside Academy. The family were very proud, with the odd exception of an aunt, uncle or cousin who thought I was getting too big for my boots. I wasn't, I really wasn't, and Mum certainly never boasted about the prizes I'd win. I just liked coming first in class, like I enjoyed coming first at running around Balgay Park during sports lessons or being on the winning side at football in the playground. Was I a bad loser? Well, I don't think so. Dad had made sure I learned about sportsmanship from an early age and I always *tried* to be generous in defeat as well as victory. It was harder though.

Joe was a prize-winner too

The down-side of being placed overall third and top boy was that it labelled me a Swot and that ensured that I'd wait a long time to be accepted by many of my schoolmates. I had a small group of friends but there was a clique of boys and girls developing who all seemed to be having fun together after school, in each other's homes in the evenings and at the weekends. I would have loved to have been invited into their circles but I knew there was absolutely no chance of that happening as long as I was top boy and the teachers' pet!

I was envious when some of the boys and girls started to pair up and I saw them holding hands at times when the teachers weren't looking. Some of the girls in our year group were very pretty indeed and I was beginning to notice it. Elissa had always been a lovely girl but I was used to her by now (well, I was due to marry her, wasn't I?) but there were one or two new faces from other primary schools who had caught my eye early on at the Annexe and for whom I took a fancy. June Barclay, a girl with a beautiful smile, kept popping into my mind at odd moments as did a certain Pauline Dunne who had the most perfect face I'd ever seen (even though her legs were unusually thin.) But some of the other girls I viewed with interest were part of the newly-formed clique of beautiful people and I didn't stand a chance there, so I scored them off the list in my head. One quite attractive wee girl was Alice Tully and I liked her a lot because she had the most extraordinary bubbly personality, always laughing and having fun. Best of all, she seemed to have no problem being openly friendly to swotty Georgie Burton. That was a nice change.

All of this girl stuff of course made me wonder whether becoming a priest could really be what I wanted to do. I was seriously considering it but kept it very much to myself and only ever talked about it to my Mum and her sisters. But it was 1966 and things were changing fast in the world, especially in terms of sex. We'd begun to hear about groups of young people called "hippies" who were living together in communes around California. They dressed extravagantly, opposed the Establishment in America, burned their draft cards for the Vietnam War and partied all the time under the influence of LSD. It was meant to make you feel really good and even see things that weren't there. Best of all, it was reported that the women often took off their clothes (tops *and* bottoms) and would do naughty things with lots of partners. Added to the glimpses of what I saw in copies of *"Mayfair"* or *"Playboy"* borrowed from pals' big brothers, my interest in Holy Orders was beginning to wobble.

Why did priests have to take a vow of celibacy anyway? I could sense deep down that that was going to complicate things for me now that I had such strong "feelings" and desperately wanted to know what this sex thing was all about. I wanted to kiss girls properly and I wanted to find out if all their chests were like the ones the women had in the magazines. The rest of it was still to some extent a mystery to many of us at the age of 12 or 13, and though I'd already had two momentary glimpses of girls, all I'd really ascertained was that they didn't have what I had down there. I knew one day I'd need to investigate further to understand what it was all about.

But as a result of all this I was beginning to suffer from the famous Catholic guilt. I suspected my thoughts were probably "bad". I knew looking at almost naked women in magazines was probably a step on the road to Hell, and sometimes it was a struggle to keep my imagination from wandering into forbidden territory. It dawned on me that priests had to be ridiculously strong-willed to resist these thoughts but it never occurred to me that maybe they didn't. Anyway, my choice was becoming stark. If I wanted to become a priest I was going to have to give up girls .... before I'd even started!

17

Papers

A paper round was pretty much essential once you were at secondary school. None of my friends had any kind of reasonably regular pocket money to spend as nobody's parents were on a salary and so they didn't bring in the same money every payday. We'd sometimes get a shilling or two from grandparents or other relatives that would help keep us in sweets, magazines, lemonade and entry to the cinema or swimming baths. As much as we'd have liked it, there was just no money tree at home. So most kids got jobs.

The figures worked like this. If I was lucky, Mum and Dad would give me a half-crown on Friday night. This was supposed to last me all week but usually it didn't even last me all weekend. As I got older, it hardly lasted me all Friday night. If things were really tight, I got nothing. But, if I was willing to get up at six o'clock in the morning, seven days a week, and deliver fifty newspapers (over a hundred on Sundays) then do the same again in the evenings (twice on Saturdays), I would earn at least seventeen shillings and sixpence plus tips. That would take me over the magic one pound threshold, which was eight times what I'd get as pocket money. What was there to consider? Of course I took a delivery round. No sensible boy could have refused unless it was more important for him to have the correct amount of sleep, be prepared and ready for school, avoid chronic back trouble, have a social life, go on holiday and generally enjoy being young and alive.

Getting up was easy. Dad was always up even earlier than me, so he would pull me out of bed before he went off to work. Once out of bed, waking up was a bit more difficult. Walking around with my brain still in neutral led to bumped heads, finding myself in closets and leaving the house ill prepared. On one occasion I reached the close at the bottom of the stairs before the chill alerted me to the fact that I was in my pyjamas, with my delivery bag slung over my shoulder. Luckily no-one was around at that ridiculous hour to see me.

But as Mum would say, there is always someone worse off than you. She was right of course. My pal Ian had a job delivering milk, which required a sleep-stealing four o'clock start, plus the courage to race around the housing estate clinging on to the back of a speeding delivery van while still only half awake. For his middle-of-the-night efforts Ian earned an obscenely generous two pounds per week, but he also had great ugly bags under his eyes and the worst late-coming record in the class. He frequently fell asleep during lessons as well, although he insisted that it was out of boredom. He may have been right.

My own delivery round covered about one mile of housing to the west of our flat, mainly on Dunholm Road which sported a mixture of tenement flats and semi-detached homes. All were rented from the Council because no-one in the immediate area owned their own house. Now, Fate had cruelly preordained that people who lived on the top floor of tenements were those most likely to want their papers delivered, so I found myself climbing four flights of stairs in almost every block of flats. I considered with envy Paper Round 1 which covered an area with no tenements at all and not a single flight of stairs to climb, but you had to be King of the paperboys to get that one. I did that round only once, when the King was sick, and it was so easy I felt I'd cheated and hadn't earned my wages.

Except in very extreme circumstances such as a broken leg, two broken legs or nuclear war, I was expected by my parents and the newsagent to turn up and do my round without complaint. Most parents treated their offspring in exactly the same manner. Neither illness nor absence from home was deemed an acceptable excuse for failure to show. Repeated painful bouts of tonsillitis did not keep me away, nor did several inches of snow, nor did staying at a friend's house. On my birthday it was no different. If I made the slightest attempt to stay in bed of a morning, I was threatened with the cold, wet sponge by my own mother, who would countenance no criticism or shame being directed at her family.

I did have the luxury of Christmas and New Year's Day off, but that was only because there were no newspapers to deliver on those days. Apart from that, I was up at five thirty and in the shop by six to check my schedule for changes. Once all the papers were safely in my bag in the order they would be delivered, it was full sack over the shoulder and out into the elements. On Sundays the luxury was verging on excessive as I had a whole extra hour in bed, but the pleasure I got from this display of sloth swiftly dissipated when I saw the enormous bag of newspapers and supplements the so-called Day of Rest heralded for me.

It certainly was a nightmare. Getting those thick, bulky broadsheets through the letter boxes was a daunting challenge in itself, and customers repeatedly complained of shredded or missing front and back pages. Nevertheless they wouldn't accept their Sunday reading being left on their doormats (it'll get nicked!) and refused to concede that a six-inch double folded wad of newsprint could not be posted through a three-inch letter box without risk of damage.

I learned from my job that the customer is always right, even when the customer is definitely wrong. How else could I have been found guilty of carelessness when Mrs. Duncan's *Courier* or *Tele* was blatantly a daily victim of her hyperactive Scotch terrier? It was obvious she could have her newspapers in one piece if she just kept darling Mickey out of the hallway or installed one of those wire mesh baskets behind the letter box. That would have made sense. But no, she insisted the paperboy had to leave her newspaper just far enough in the letter box to hold it there, but not enough to allow Mickey to reach it. Boy, that dog was determined. I could picture Mrs. Duncan coming out into the hallway on her morning trek to the loo, and being horrified to find her beloved pooch hanging by the teeth from a folded copy of the *Sunday Post*.

Almost all of my customers took the four publications of D.C.Thompson, our local newspaper magnates: the *Courier & Advertiser,* the *Evening Telegraph*, the *Sporting Post* (Saturday evenings only) and the world famous *Sunday Post*, which we were told was flown to every corner of the planet. Dundee's daily morning and evening papers tended to have much the same local news and stories, but very few folk preferred the west-coast flavoured reporting of the Daily Record and Sunday Mail.

I only ever blotted my copybook once as a paperboy. A combination of tonsillitis, recent school exams and torrential rain left me weak and shaky as I arrived soaking wet at the newsagent's. Of course it had to be a Sunday as well. I went into the shop to find a mountain of supplements, free gifts, pull-out extras and various trial offers to be added to the already bulging two bags I was expected to carry. I struggled with my preparations but eventually I was ready to leave. The newsagent hurried me back outside into the rain with a sympathetic "Don't hang about" and pushed me off in the direction of my first delivery. I never made it. Somewhere near the entrance to the very first close, my burden seemed to become unbearably heavy and I sank to the ground in a great puddle of rain. I don't know how long I sat there but a kind pensioner found me and returned me to the paper shop. The newsagent drove me home and I spent the rest of that Sunday in bed. The following morning I was up at six for work. Mum said I had to.

18

Sixty-Six

Before I knew it, my first year at secondary school was drawing to a close. It had indeed lived up to all expectations, what with moving from the Annexe and then getting to know loads of new teachers and new friends. My success at coming third in first year was the icing on the cake. Admittedly I'd been on the receiving end of a few beltings, some merited, some not, as well as the odd hurtful comment about how thin I was or what a swot I was, but overall the experience had been brilliant and I felt I had become a real Lawsider as kids at the other schools called us. They also had alternative names that weren't quite so polite.

Joe had had a pretty good fourth year as well, winning the prize for English, his story called *"Teatime under the Yellow August Moon"* getting rave reviews in the School Magazine, and becoming a bit of a hit with the girls. I put that down to his good fortune in having long, blond, wavy hair which the fairer sex seemed to find attractive. I of course couldn't really see why this should set him apart from his peers when his pal Albin was much more exciting and had very long ginger hair, but there was no denying that these days dear brother Joe was spending a lot of his time in female company. He was also grinning a good deal more in a way that reminded me of Yvonne and Rover the dog.

I was aware that going out with a girl included kissing and cuddling and holding hands, for which pleasures boys, like Joe, would "pay her in" to the cinema, the dancing, the ice rink with its cool music or even the theatre. Being a lover of language and all things literary, as well as of females, Joe had started to attend shows at Dundee Repertory Theatre, especially when there was a Shakespearean drama on offer. It appeared that girls really liked that sort of thing too.

On the verge of sixteen, Joe had also been initiated long since to the wonders of drinking alcohol. I had observed at first hand on more than one occasion how this substance affected my brother's ability to talk and walk. He tried very hard to disguise these effects when he first got home on weekend evenings and had to spend an outrageously long two minutes telling Mum where and with whom he'd been spending time. I'm sure the ridiculous slurring of his words was a dead giveaway but Mum seemed to be happy that he had come home safely in one piece, especially if he'd chosen for company a good Catholic girl. But good Catholic girlfriends tended to have high standards and one such lass promptly ended her liaison with him when he rather impolitely vomited all over her feet as they snuggled up in the bus on a school trip to the Wallace Monument in Stirling. Clearly that

156

hadn't been purely orange squash in the bottle he'd been sipping from.

He had also taken to smoking cigarettes. This was no surprise as Mum smoked a pack of Wills' Woodbine a day and our house was permanently filled with a pall of tobacco smoke. So were most of the homes in the family and in those of my friends. Cousin Peter, the budding pop star, didn't smoke, but he didn't need to enhance his image with a fag when he was already a singer and lead guitarist. It wouldn't be an exaggeration to say that almost all the other people I knew in Dundee smoked cigarettes, yet there was talk of it being very bad for your health, and the Government had even banned the advertising of cigarettes on TV in the previous year.

I hadn't moved on from puffing cinnamon sticks at that point so I'd never really smoked, although I'd come close, especially on dark nights out in the back green of 44 Prince's Croft with my "decadent" Coupar Angus cousins Wee Mary and Renée. They both smoked like chimneys as did most of the girls of their age. When these two sat down with Auntie Mary their mother to play Knock-out Whist with my Mum Peggy and Auntie Katie, the five of them would create a cloud of smoke worthy of a factory chimney. I would sit in the midst of this fug and not even notice. Joe fell victim to our girl cousins' trendiness by agreeing to let them practise applying a false tan on him. It was somewhat less than successful, but Joe made it a lot worse by trying to bluff everyone at school that he'd just been to Majorca. I don't think many people believed him.

In 1966 the first three weeks of the summer holidays were spent as usual at the berry-picking. We were all pretty good pickers by then but unfortunately the weather was fairly rainy that year and our bonus income was somewhat stop-start. My pals and I found ourselves passing more and more time down in the city centre looking for ways to spend what berry money we had. Each time we'd go to the Central Baths we were greeted by spectacular changes to Dundee's waterfront. In the course of three years, three of the docks through which Joe and I had walked so many weekends to go swimming or fishing had been filled in. This transformation meant they even had to move the famous warship HMS Unicorn to a more eastern dock, and almost out of sight.

For me, the most drastic change to that part of the city had been the demolition of the massive Victoria Arch, which had dominated the waterfront opposite Shore Terrace bus station since Queen Victoria had visited Dundee. The removal of this iconic gateway had raised controversy all around Dundee, but the city planners got their way and the huge blackened gate disappeared when I was still in Primary 7. Now, at thirteen, I hardly recalled this irreplaceable landmark or the three once-thriving docks. Progress and the modernisation of our city were inevitable, and Dundee would soon be looking magnificently modern.

The Royal Arch comes crashing down

(Used by kind permission of DC Thomson & Co Ltd)

The whole country was expanding. There were New Towns which had sprung up all over the place, built to modern designs. East Kilbride was the first near us and it was vaunted in the press as a shining example of post-war progress. The little town of Linwood in Renfrewshire boasted a car assembly line, producing the Hillman Imp. Glenrothes was also expected to change the image of the Kingdom of Fife forever. Cousin Pat, younger brother of Joe Casciani, had moved to Glenrothes shortly after his wedding to Marion, and they had even bought their own house in Sinclair Avenue. This had sent ripples of envy through the family. There was only one other person I knew who lived in a house that wasn't rented from the Council. Times were indeed changing fast.

How strange that on 30 July of that year I found myself in that very house in Glenrothes for possibly the only time in my life. Mum, Dad, Joe and I had crossed the Tay on the Scotscraig *"Fifie"*, one of the River Tay ferry-boats, and had gone by Bluebird bus to Glenrothes to visit Pat and Marion. However, once we got there we spent most of the afternoon in front of the TV. My Dad had insisted that we tune in to the BBC, but then so did 30 million others! The football World Cup Final was being televised from Wembley.

England led but the Germans snatched an equaliser in the last seconds. Then in extra-time Geoff Hurst crashed the ball off the bar and down onto the goal line: the referee awarded a contentious goal to England, but it became academic when, with only seconds remaining, Hurst ran clear again and sent the third of his hat-trick past a static German goalkeeper. Dad was jumping up and down with delight. In truth we were all really happy that the

English had won. We just didn't realise they would never stop talking about it.

Pat and Marion

In August we had a visit from Uncle Jud and family, nine of us piling into his wee van and scooting off on trips to St. Andrews, Broughty Ferry, Arbroath and Carnoustie. The weather was quite kind to us, with a reasonable amount of warm sunshine, so we inevitably all got sunburnt and spent a few uncomfortable nights trying to sleep standing up. Mum smothered our bright red skins in calamine lotion and it helped but didn't entirely spare us from the agonies of touching things. It wasn't helped by us kids having to sleep three and two to a bed, Paul and me in with Joe, Maria and little Maureen in my bed.

A day at Broughty Ferry beach

Just after they returned to Leeds for the rest of their break, our school holidays came to an end and we went back to a now familiar Lawside Academy, me into second year and Joe into fifth. His "O Grade" results had arrived in the brown envelope just a few days before and he'd done very well so he'd be sitting a handful of Highers at the end of this academic year. At registration on the very first day my own class was greeted by a new teacher, a young man in his early twenties, well-built, sporty and with a great big smile on his face.

162

He introduced himself as the new P.E. teacher Mr Chaplain. None of us had any idea at that moment how very important this man was going to be to us.

"Jimmy" Chaplain was one of a new breed of teachers who had learned that it was mutually beneficial to teacher and pupil alike to strike up a positive relationship. For the teacher this was quite revolutionary, as it meant getting to know the pupils not only personally but with knowledge of their backgrounds, families, hobbies and future aspirations. For us in 2A Boys, Jimmy broke the mould of the distant, aloof masters who avoided personal relationships and believed that wasn't part of the job. Mr. Chaplain became much more than a Register teacher. He was there at every turn, helping us to avoid trouble with good, sound advice and kicking our behinds when they needed kicking. We all thought he was wonderful.

But the first great event of my second year didn't happen at school. No, it took place down by the river when the Tay Road Bridge was opened on 18 August by the Queen Mother. Hers was the first car to cross the mile-and-a-half long bridge from the very centre of Dundee at Shore Terrace to the coast of Fife between Newport and Tayport. Thousands followed her car across, taking advantage of the toll holiday that only lasted 4 days before the princely sum of 2/6d was required each way to get you over the water. The opening of the beautiful white bridge was another sign of the massive progress Dundee was making, and many motorists went out of their way simply to have the thrill of driving over the mighty River Tay.

Mum, Grandma from Leeds and Dad on the "Fifie"

Sadly, the arrival of the bridge heralded the departure of the *"Fifies"* that had transported cars, lorries, cyclists and foot passengers across to Fife and back for the previous 50 years. The very last crossing took place the day the bridge was opened and that was the last I ever saw of those brilliant vessels. I knew I would remember my fun on board during the many crossings I'd made with Mum and Dad before the diesel-driven ferries retired to the island of Malta. They were badly missed by many of the townspeople of Dundee.

Back in the football world, there was a major sensation when wee Dundee United competed in the Inter Cities Fairs Cup tournament, their first time in a European competition. Astonishingly they were paired with Spanish giants Barcelona in the second round, after a bye in the first. What a shock travelled around Europe when United not only beat them 2-1 in the cauldron of the Nou Camp but repeated the dose with a thumping 2-0 victory back at Tannadice Park in Dundee. The city's name was even further enhanced. Even when United crashed out to Juventus in the very next round, nobody would remember that defeat, only the glory of two wonderful victories over Barcelona.

And so the town and the country in general continued on a bit of a high and there was a lot of optimism in the press and in the pubs. Everything seemed to be moving in the right direction within the family as well, with cousin Tony and cousin Wee Mary both getting married. There was a genuine sense of happiness about the place. Of course, there was still the war in Vietnam, but we weren't involved in that so it did little to dampen the nation's spirits. But dour Mum said something bad was bound to happen …… and it did.

On the morning of 21 October, after weeks of heavy rain, a slipping spoil tip above the mining village of Aberfan in Wales suddenly engulfed part of the town, including the local school. 144 people died in that awful catastrophe, 116 of them children. This tragic accident pulled us all up sharp. How was it possible? How could so many innocent children go off to school and never come home? Tears were shed for these poor souls all over the country, and people flocked to churches to offer prayers. That's the bit that got to me.

You see, I'd spent the previous seven years believing firmly in a loving God, whose son Jesus Christ so loved us that he sacrificed himself on a cross to bring us to eternal salvation. His love for us was supposed to be limitless. So what was Aberfan all about? If he loved those kids so much, how could he let them be buried alive beneath a coal tip? I thought about this a lot, and I wasn't the only one. Teachers at Lawside tried to give us an explanation we could understand, but I remained unconvinced by what they said and I just couldn't square that tragedy in Wales with a definition of God as kind and loving.

By Christmas of 1966, I had given up any intention of becoming a priest.

19

Luck

Auntie Katie wasn't the only one in the family to win on the pools. She got three thousand pounds when I was about ten, but Dad won too, and coincidentally it was me again who checked the coupon. I suppose that was to be expected as, after Katie's win, I was regarded as the lucky checker. Regularly I'd be called upon by various members of the family to open tickets, choose bingo cards, draw lots, spin wheels of fortune and anything else that required the intervention of a boy with some lucky dust in his hair.

On our way to England with Auntie Katie

On Grand National day each year Mum insisted I pick a couple of horses for her to back, maybe because she thought that my random selections would have as good a chance of winning as the ones so many adults spent hours analysing.

Back in 1963 Mum and Dad had boiled their statistics down to just one horse with any chance of winning. That horse was called *Team Spirit* and Dad started using the dangerous phrase "a dead cert" about it, because in his view it would definitely win the National. Having assisted with Auntie Katie's win, I was asked by Mum to cast my enchanted eye over the list of runners. Right away I pointed to a horse called Ayala which sounded exotic to me and therefore, obviously to me, would be the best horse in the race. Dad checked the odds on my selection and saw it was a rank outsider at 66/1, so he laughed and told Mum not to waste another sixpence. Mum refused to be swayed, and she was no stranger to obstinacy. She put sixpence each-way on my horse. Ayala squeezed home at the last gasp that year, scooping Mum a cool two pounds in profit, while Dad's "dead-cert" trailed in fourth. He was right though. Team Spirit *did* win the Grand National.....but that was the following year when Dad had invested elsewhere.

When I was thirteen, it wasn't just correctly predicting eight draws that won you money on Littlewoods' or Vernon's football pools. You could also play the Points Pool every week as well. This required you to predict the outcome of twelve selected games: home win, away win or draw. The pay-out was determined by how many other people also guessed correctly. If you were the only one in the country to get all twelve right then there was a big bag of money heading for your address, and in Dundee in those days that could change a life. Dad had a method of picking nine games where he predicted a specific outcome and three games at which he could afford to have more than one guess. This made the stake more expensive because of the number of permutations involved but, as each of them could cost less than a penny, he still wasn't spending very much.

That Saturday, having assumed the position in front of the TV, I ticked off the draws on the front of Dad's coupon and announced as usual that he didn't have quite enough to give up his job on the buses. I then turned the coupon over and checked the results of the teams on the Points Pools. I was so excited to tell him that he had eleven results correct, though everything still rested on Scunthorpe v Crewe Alexandra. Yet Dad leapt up and shouted out in delight that he'd won, grabbing Mum in his arms and spinning her around. Mum got quite flustered and tried to wriggle free, but Dad was ecstatic. I tried again to tell him he only had eleven correct and needed one more before celebration, but he just grinned more widely. Then he told me to check his prediction for the

Scunthorpe game once more. It was only then that I saw he had all three possible results penned alongside that particular game. He was indeed right. It wouldn't matter how that game finished, he was bound to be in the money.

Let joy be unbounded! Well, not for all of us. Mum remained her usual stoic self, already worrying over possible chaotic events that could stop the win being confirmed. Maybe the agent had absconded with the stake money or perhaps Dad's copy had a mistake in it. Dad, Joe and I were a lot less restrained, running around the flat, jumping up and down, hugging each other in a way Dad didn't normally indulge in, and generally making a lot of noise. Only a knock at the door halted our celebrations and, as it was grumpy Mrs Barnett from downstairs complaining about the racket we were making, that was the end of the frivolity. Dad sobered up and apologised, but then assured her we would never again disturb her peace by winning the pools. That was possibly the wittiest thing I ever heard him say.

The Evening Telegraph the following Wednesday announced that a penny per line stake on the Points Pools won you nearly three thousand two hundred pounds. That's not what Dad got though, because he had only staked a quarter penny per line, meaning he'd receive a quarter of the pot, or approximately eight hundred pounds. As that amount of money represented six months' wages for Dad in those days, he was a very happy bus driver.

The first luxury item paid for by his good fortune was a twin tub washing machine to take some strain off Mum. It didn't take *much* strain off Mum as she still had to lift steaming hot clothes out of the washing compartment with her wooden tongs and stuff them into the narrow spin compartment. But compared to the daily toil of squeezing freshly-washed clothes through a mangle clamped to the sink then hanging them out on the washing line, I suppose she thought the twin tub was a great improvement and a real labour-saving device.

Joe and I were far more interested in the second purchase – the new television. That put us up there with our poshest friends and made it much more likely they'd accept our offers of tea or an overnight stay. In a way it also hammered the last nail in the coffin lid of cinema for us as the highlight of family entertainment. Why venture out on a cold, wet evening and pay to see a giant version of what you could watch for free from your armchair? It was as if we had a miniature cinema in our living-room. We might not get the latest films but we had *"Dr. Kildare"* and lots of equally gory entertainment.

We entered the world of the future a bit later when Dad had piped television installed in the flat, cutting out the need for an aerial on the roof, as the signal came through a cable right into the living-room.

From then on we had uninterrupted viewing even on the snowiest or windiest of evenings and Mum was soon warning Joe and me that we would get square eyes if we watched any more TV. The STV signal came down our pipe instead of the Grampian TV one and this was significant later on when STV started showing live football games that weren't available on the other commercial channel. On those evenings our house was packed full of friends and relations enjoying the action while Mum was kept busy with the teas and lemonades.

Despite my anointed reputation as a bringer of good fortune, I seemed to be particularly unlucky at cards. Mum and I still played most Friday nights while Dad and Joe were out doing whatever they were doing. I rarely felt confident about asking for a further card at *Pontoon* as it was invariably a face card, taking me past the twenty-one maximum to result in a Bust. It did no good that she consoled me with the certainty that, if I was unlucky at cards, I would be lucky in love. This did very little to lighten my disappointment as I failed to see how you'd be lucky in love unless you married a girl who owned a sweet shop.

Dad used his pools win to treat us to a holiday that summer. This was a real holiday, in a boarding-house in Scarborough where Mum didn't have to cook or clean. Dad even hired a brand new Ford Consul to take us there. Now that was very special because, as a bus driver, he had no desire to spend any of his free-time driving any vehicle whatsoever. We all knew exactly what a "busman's holiday" meant. But that year we zoomed off to the Yorkshire coast for a whole week's pampering. Or so we thought. Within minutes of our arrival a huge unsmiling woman with a trace of a beard was reading us out a long list of things we weren't allowed to do, removing any hope I had of enjoying myself for one minute under her roof. Thankfully breathing was not on the list but eating and drinking were, unless it was in her spotless dining-room, and only then at very specific hours. Joe and

I weren't really bothered too much about the restrictions as we were outside most of the time, but Mum was utterly terrified of that lady and wore her characteristic frown the whole time we were there. At least I found it fun in the dining-room at meal times, when all the guests ate at the same time and tried to have really quiet conversations, which only made the scene funnier. I checked the list again. Speaking wasn't on it, but the adults acted as if it were.

On the day we left, the bearded lady raced us through breakfast, gave us a generous thirty minutes to get our cases packed and into the car, and was preparing to hoover our room before we'd even left it. On the way out I added "having fun" to her long list of things that guests were not allowed to do.

My long-term interest in backing the horses didn't come from Dad's almost daily punt but from that rogue of rogues, my cousin Tony Brown. He wasn't just interested in horse-racing, he was absolutely addicted to it, so as I had, since about the age of eight, thought that the sun shone from his rear end, it was natural that I should become the Tipster's Apprentice. Very often when we were together, Tony would produce the newspaper, turn it to the racing section and instruct me in the mysteries of how to read the form guide.

Tony and Sandra's wedding

He'd also show me his racing ledger, an old accounts book in which he had faithfully written the results of all the most important races year on year. He had recorded the horse, jockey, trainer, weight and starting price of the 1-2-3 of all the Classics and the other big prizes. Then, when he got older and no longer could be bothered with all that writing, he passed the ledger on to me and said I should keep it up-to-date. And of course I did. By the age of thirteen, I knew the names of the winners of the Derby, Grand National, One Thousand and Two Thousand Guineas, the Oaks, the St. Leger and several other big races from 1950 onwards. Mum used to test me on a quiet evening and that helped me get even better at remembering. This was a very useful memory exercise that certainly paid off in later life.

Luck was also on my side in the early Sixties when Dad started taking me along to Dens Park to see Dundee F.C. play. Not only did the Dark Blues win the Scottish League, but they also had a fantastic run to the semi-finals of the European Cup. Dad and I were there on the Provost Road terracing as the mighty Cologne, Sporting Lisbon and Anderlecht were duly dispatched by Alan Gilzean and Co. We also saw them beat the legendary A.C. Milan at Dens Park, though they lost to the Italians on aggregate. Standing in crowds of 45,000 when just a youngster and having to climb the base of the floodlights to see the game, gave me a love of football that I never lost.

Dundee F.C. '61-'62 (used with kind permission of D C Thompson Ltd)

20

Names

Now in second year at Lawside, I had long since ceased being known as *'Wee Georgie Burton'* and was addressed in one of three ways. To my teachers I was "Burton" whether said nicely or not, although Jimmy Chaplain was starting to use our Christian names and reserving our surnames for when he was displeased with us. To my Mum, Dad, cousins, aunts and uncles, I was just plain "Georgie". To my classmates "Georgie" was beginning to morph into "George" but that was pronounced with the Dundonians' healthy contempt for normal vowels that made it into "Joe-rge".

OK, a Perth lad called Peter Kaye did call me "Dode" on occasions and, although this title didn't stick, he never called me by my given name. For a while I got fed up being George and asked all my pals to call me Gerry, which I thought was a much cooler label and was a shortened version of my middle name. A good idea maybe, but no-one could remember to stop calling me Joe-rge, so Gerry just never caught on.

I was far from alone in having variations to my name. New pal Lawrence Donnachie immediately became "Dodge" on the entirely logical basis that

Lawrence shortened to Lawrie and as so many lorries were made by the firm Dodge, then "Dodge" it would be ever after. Allan Flood's nickname was logic itself – "Splash"! Michael Docherty was of course "Doc" while Eric McCabe, another Perth boy, spent his entire secondary school career known as "Ilya" because of an astounding resemblance to the Russian Ilya Kuryakin in the spy series *"The Man from U.N.C.L.E."* Paul Van der Boon became "Vanders" or "PVB" depending on who was speaking about him. My pal Peter McLaren was christened straight out of the *Beano*. No, he wasn't Dennis or Snooty, he was one of the Bash Street Kids. We called him Plug.

Nicknames were almost entirely the preserve of the boys at school and only one girl was not called by her Christian name. For some obscure reason Eileen Beck only ever got called "Beck". My personal favourite nickname was the one I helped establish when playing football over the field on South Road. One lad from a few closes up the road was Ian Webster, a year or so younger than me, and his name Ian was gradually replaced by "Cooch" after I spotted his passing resemblance to Coochee Bear on a TV show. The teachers at Lawside of course had their fair share of nicknames too. The diminutive Head of English, Mr. Ferrie, was known as "Tich" while his always perfectly-dressed colleague Mr. McIntosh was "Mac the Mod". Jimmy Chaplain often went by the name of

"Chappy", Mr. Mahoney from Languages was "Slip" (Goodness knows why), Mr. Paterson was "Piggy", Mr. Devine was "Gummer" and Mr. Adams the Headmaster was always called "Ted". And so the list went on. Probably the cleverest nickname was the one awarded to the Head of Classics, Mr. Burns. His bald head naturally meant everyone knew him as "Eggo", but the name was also a brilliant pun on the Latin word Ego for "I".

Many of my teachers appeared here

TV was beginning to dominate our evenings at home. While Mum wouldn't miss a single episode of *"Coronation Street"*, *"Peyton Place"*, *"Crossroads"* or *"Z Cars"*, Dad had a particular liking for a war series called *"Hogan's Heroes"*. Joe and I were of course huge fans of *"Top of the Pops"* with a chance of seeing our own musical heroes, but we were also big fans of *"The Monkees"*, a crazy show from America featuring four young musicians modelled not too subtly on our Beatles, doing mad things and singing their songs. Another show from America that made us laugh was *"The Beverly Hillbillies"* with oil millionaire Jed Clampett and his family causing mayhem in upmarket Los Angeles. We particularly liked his tomboy daughter Elly Mae, played by the absolutely gorgeous Donna Douglas. Joe was also an avid fan of that strange series, *"The Prisoner"* but I couldn't understand it.

Television took a big step forward later that school session with the introduction of colour via new sets with 625 lines as opposed to the old 405 lines ours had. We'd seen the coloured test-card at Auntie Mary's house and it looked brilliant so we were hoping that we'd soon be able to afford one. As usual, we'd have to be patient and continue for now to watch the world in black and white. And what a world it was turning into. There were half a million US troops fighting Communism in Vietnam, the boxing hero Muhammad Ali was put in jail for refusing to fight there, British farming was devastated by an outbreak of Foot & Mouth disease, and Israel had a short but vicious war with Egypt. We seemed to be pretty safe living in Dundee, but once we heard that China had tested a hydrogen bomb, we realised that nowhere was really safe and never would be again.

Thankfully there were things to cheer us all up in music and sport, and not just the wonderful goings-on in Scottish football. Francis Chichester successfully sailed single-handedly around the whole world, and returned in triumph to Plymouth to a fantastic reception before being made a Knight. But it was music that was unbelievably vibrant as my second year at school came to a close. While other bands strove to challenge their supremacy, the Beatles brought out a studio album of innovative songs on the first day of June. *"Sergeant Pepper's Lonely Hearts Club Band"* was intricate and wonderful, and it's a lovely thought that I was around at the time to listen to what I believe was the most important album in the history of modern music.

21

Indoors

Dad really liked table tennis because he thought he was great at it. He claimed to have beaten Mum a hundred games on the trot and put this remarkable run of victories down to his vicious spinning serve. The truth was that Mum was useless at all sports and had the eye-to-ball coordination of a blindfolded drunk. I knew why Dad won so often: it was simply because he was left-handed. That put you off a lot, especially when he served. At the time, I found it strange that Dad was a southpaw in sports like darts and tennis but wrote with his right hand. I eventually found out that he wanted to write with his left hand as a child, but had been absolutely forbidden by teachers who determined to rid him of his "handicap".

The folding dining-table was the venue for our regular table tennis matches and it served the purpose quite well, except for its rounded corners which caught an inordinate percentage of shots and sent the ball flying off at sharp and irretrievable angles. In the early years at South Road the game sometimes came to a premature conclusion when the ball shot off the corner of the table and landed perfectly in the middle of the coal fire, where it melted to nothing. For a long time we either had only one bat or none at all, but this didn't prevent us from enjoying the family tournament. Mum had discovered that her hardback copy of "Treasure Island" doubled as a rather fine table tennis bat. She even used it at times when a real bat was available. She was of course then able to blame the lack of proper equipment for her innumerable defeats by Dad, Joe and me. A level playing field was only re-established if there was an accidental breakage of the one bat we had, in which case Mum's opponent had to avail himself of "Swiss Family Robinson" or "Kidnapped".

Three equal-sized books standing with raised horizontal spines also served as the net when circumstances dictated, allowing us to play away happily at table tennis with nothing but a dining-table, a ball and five books. My parents' skills of improvisation were remarkable and a source of inspiration for Joe and me. Dad even had the ability to rescue the ball if it went under someone's foot and emerged with a dent in it. He would simply strike a match and hold it under the unfortunate dimpled ball, displaying awesome ingenuity as the plastic expanded and the dent disappeared. Wonderful!

There was however and as ever a downside to these idyllic family evenings indoors. Because the table had to be placed between the back of the settee and the sideboard, there was very little space on either side although plenty room at each end where the players stood. Consequently, objects placed on the sideboard ran a serious risk of being knocked over by an outstretched bat as one player would try to defend a diagonal smash in that direction. Over the years we damaged numerous ornaments, clocks, framed photos and trinkets.

My most shameful moment came one winter's evening when I swiped wildly to return Joe's searing volley and cleanly removed the Madonna's head from a decorated bottle of Lourdes water. Mum was not best pleased. Nor was my dear big brother the night I swatted backhand at a smash from Dad down my left-hand side and connected fully with the top of Joe's head as he sat on the settee watching "The Avengers". Add to that the black eye Mum got from the ball when Dad accidentally whacked it straight at her and the chip Joe took out of the table when he mistimed a low service return, and it is easy to understand why our table-tennis evenings weren't always the family bonding sessions they were meant to be.

Our other favourite indoor pastime was Bagatelle. Now this game really was fun. The board was about three feet long by two feet wide, had little legs at the far end to create the requisite slope, and a pull-back spring-loaded launcher that fired a ball bearing (or a marble if we lost the ball bearing) up the channel and out into the scoring zone. This forerunner of pinball had little nails hammered into the board, to send the balls off in different directions and at different angles.

The Bagatelle board (used with kind permission of Jaques of London)

On each turn there were three possibilities. The ball could enter one of several cages that awarded different scores, it could drop into a recess in the floor of the board which also carried a score, or it could score zero by falling all the way to the bottom without landing in either. We tried endlessly to drop the ball into the cage with the maximum 150 which was tucked away in an almost inaccessible place near the bottom. Needless to say, we didn't succeed very often, but it was fun trying.

Other evenings were often dedicated to a family game of cards as well. Mum called them "the devil's cards" as they frequently led to quarrels at the end of the evening. We were all ever so competitive. Learning to be a good loser was really, really hard for me, and storming off to the bedroom so no-one could see the tears in my eyes was a typical ending to an evening of good, clean fun with Mum, Dad and Joe. We played loads of different card games such as 9-card brag, whist, gin rummy, switch and lots more, but our favourite was definitely "Newmarket" or "Horsey-Horsey" as Auntie Mary called it.

There were two ways of winning the 'pot' in the game of "Newmarket". You either had to be the first to play all the cards in your hand or you had to have played the king of the suit of the secret card placed face-down during every deal. Winning both in one hand was brilliant, especially if the secret card had rolled over a couple of times, allowing you to scoop two or three or even four times the normal cache of matchsticks. It was always matchsticks, not money. Mum wasn't keen on the gambling aspect of the game, even though she backed the horses every time the Grand National came round. And yet we played the games as if each match was a gold ingot of incredible value. The overall winner would count out their haul of Swan Vestas or Bluebell matches like a high-roller playing the tables in Monte-Carlo. We all hated not to win.

Then one day other indoor sports entered our lives. This is how it happened. At about teatime a Corporation double-decker bus pulled up right outside our block though we weren't on a bus route. I was astonished to see my Dad jump down from the driver's cabin and make his way round to the entrance platform at the rear, disappearing inside into the lower deck. Within seconds all the little kids from the immediate flats were milling around the bus, asking if they could get on board. Dad must have said OK because several of them leapt onto the platform and dashed up the stairs to the top deck, filling the front seats and pretending they were driving. I opened the living-room window to get a clearer view and could hear the bell being rung over and over again but, surprisingly, there were no complaints from either Dad or his conductor.

When both of them came back into view they were carrying on their shoulders what looked like a long thick tube wrapped in plastic. They disappeared down the stairs and into the close, so I ran to open the front door, keen to find out what they were bringing. As Dad reached the top of the stairs he shooed me out of the way and snaked his way into the lobby with Charlie the conductor still bringing up the rear. The two of them eventually eased the heavy object to the floor, hands were shaken, and with a wave they both set off back downstairs. I went through to the living-room window to watch them get back on the bus after chasing away the

187

local ragamuffins, and off they drove noisily as Dad crashed through the uncooperative low gears.

Back inside, Mum set to work on the plastic wrapping with the big pinking shears, gradually revealing a dark blue carpet. How classy was that? We were going to have our own carpet, our very first. The high life was reaching the edges of old Dundee! It would be cheerio to the cold linoleum which floored the entire flat. I was unbelievably proud. But I wondered why our carpet had been delivered in a Corporation bus and not a carpet van. Mum suggested that maybe all the carpet vans had been busy and she quickly changed the subject to the question of whether or not I had finished my homework. She knew I had, because I always did my homework quickly as soon as I got home from school. Perhaps she was remembering my proclivity to tell too much to other people....

During tea that evening my parents talked about nothing else, discussing where the carpet should be laid, how many rooms it might cover and what to do about underlay. The latter point was quickly cleared up by Mum. She said there'd be nothing better than layers of newspaper to cushion, soundproof and stop the carpet's foam back from sticking to the linoleum, which was to be left in place. The Dundee Courier & Advertiser would serve yet another purpose in the local community. After we'd had tea Dad, Joe and I manhandled the carpet into different rooms where we tried to

188

spread it out as best we could without moving the furniture. Soon the sweat was lashing from all three of us, so Joe fetched a twelve-inch ruler from his school bag and measured the carpet's length and width then the dimensions of each room. That approach saved us a lot of labour.

We now sat round the dining-table while Dad and Joe worked out which rooms could be covered by such a long, rather narrow carpet. I asked why Dad hadn't bought one that fitted but Joe just smacked my head and told me to shut up. Dad raised his eyes to heaven and went back to the maths. Eventually we worked out that the carpet could cover Mum and Dad's bedroom (if they missed out the area below the bed) and most of the lobby, except the bit behind the front door. Several cuts and joins would be required but Dad was supremely confident he could rise to the occasion. He did do a terrific job of laying the carpet the next day, despite ruining a pair of Mum's scissors in the process. Joe and I spent the whole evening wrestling on the carpet or walking up and down the lobby with no shoes on and great big grins on our faces. At last we were posh.

The arrival of the carpet curtailed the table-tennis tournaments a bit because we now had a perfect putting green in our lobby. This game quickly became the family pastime of choice. We spent many a Friday evening imagining the eighteenth hole at St. Andrews as we used a scavenged old putter to aim our ball at a recumbent pint glass. When the weekend pubs closed at ten, Dad would come home and show us how it was done left-handed. Even with a few pints on him (it being Friday night), he was still so much better than Mum, Joe or me. Mum was next best and I soon became her usual opponent as Joe decided he was too busy with other things to risk being beaten at a sport by his mother.

The blue carpet introduced another game into the house, this time mainly for Joe and me. It was balloon football. Suddenly it was ok to lie on my back and roll around on the lobby floor, being a strange slow-motion goalkeeper, trying to save slow-motion headers from my slow-motion brother. The weirdest part was that we both liked to commentate on our games with slow-motion speech, lengthening the vowels of key words like "save" and "goal" to fit the speed of the actions they were describing.

Honestly, it didn't seem surreal at the time.

22

Gym

I loved my P.E. lessons at school. One of the teachers, Mr. Devlin, was a bit fierce but I knew if you stayed on the right side of him there was no problem. The other gym teachers, Chaplain and Pacione, were fine with us, meaning we all looked forward to their lessons. There were three kinds of activity we did. We had outdoor team games and athletics on the playing fields next to the Kingsway, or indoor games and gymnastics in the big gymnasium, or swimming in our brand-new pool. I loved all three sorts but especially looked forward to an organised game of football on the playing field, even on rainy days if the teachers felt brave enough to take us there. Sometimes a good old Dundee downpour would persuade them to change their plans at the last minute, and we'd double up with some other class in the gym instead of facing the elements.

The swimming pool was a top attraction not only because it was ours to use in our own school and required no travelling to get there, but also because the water was really warm in comparison to both the Central and Lochee Baths. As the pool was on the school site, it was also possible to go swimming at lunch time or after school. Some of us would take advantage of this facility, even though we had to do real swimming of lengths, up and down, as opposed to the horseplay we usually got up to in the public pools. Diving in or doing a "depth charge" was regarded as a bit too disruptive for school, where we were expected to behave ourselves and get on with becoming competent swimmers.

It was in that school swimming pool that I found myself totally changing my opinion about one of the teachers. Mr. Minto, known to us as "Wullie", was the Latin teacher for second year and he came very much from the old-fashioned school of teaching. He wore the black gown of a graduate and talked to us very formally at all times. He never seemed to smile yet wasn't particularly grumpy, paraded around the room with his book held out in front of him and, when the bell rang at the end of the lesson, would immediately announce above the rising noise "Right, for homework ......" We would moan loudly because this meant we then had to take out our homework registers and write in whatever he told us to do: no chance of a quick escape there.

As a result of his standoffishness, we all regarded him as a bit of a wimp and treated him with less respect than his lessons deserved, given that he didn't often use the belt and was never really nasty to anyone. We fourteen-year olds just preferred to be taught by someone with a bit more charisma than Mr. Minto, that's all, and his only fault was that he was from a dying breed. But he was generally a nice man despite his formality.

My impression of him started changing at the pool during the after-school session we sometimes attended. As I came out of the showers I noticed a figure surging powerfully through the water away from me. I was even more impressed by the swimmer's perfect somersault turn at the deep end before he came crashing back towards where I'd stopped at the poolside. When he reached my feet, off he went again. He cut through the water like an Olympic swimmer, doing length after length non-stop at the same terrific speed. I couldn't make out who he was, as I couldn't really see his face and I didn't recognise his muscular frame as he leapt from the water when he'd had enough.

But the next time I saw him cutting up and down the pool like a fish, I waited at the shallow end to try to identify him. Imagine my shock when he finished his final length, stood up to display muscles on top of more muscles, then pulled off his expensive-looking goggles. Surely it couldn't be who I thought it was? Yes, there was no doubt at this close range. It was Wullie Minto, the unassuming teacher of the Latin class. I half expected him to announce what I had for homework! So my respect for him soared. Underneath his graduate's cloak, he had the kind of body all of us boys hoped to have by the age of eighteen, and most of us would never be able to swim a quarter as well as he could.

He showed his true colours the day Sinky Sinclair pushed his luck too far in Latin class and completely disrupted the lesson. Sinky became so aggressive that Mr. Minto had to drag him out of the door. We listened in amazement to the sounds of a struggle outside on the landing then we were surprised when Mr. Minto came back in, calmly closed the door behind him, picked up his text book from the floor and continued with "Right, for homework ......" At that instant, Sinky came crashing back in and made for Mr. Minto with serious menace on his face. We all knew how dangerous Sinky could be, many of us from painful experience, so we expected the worst. Astonishingly, as Sinky reached him, the teacher performed some kind of lightning-fast fighting manoeuvre that left our bullying classmate on the floor with his arm twisted up his back, and the teacher's knee keeping him firmly face down. Someone was sent for assistance and a much quieter Sinky was removed. We looked differently at Wullie Minto after that. We eventually found out that our Latin master had done loads of Commando training.

I had one reservation about doing gym. I didn't mind climbing the wall bars of which there were many and I put up with the trial of pulling myself up to the top of one of the six thick, white ropes that hung from the ceiling. I took on with relish vaulting the big box via the miniature trampoline and doing some kind of somersault, hopefully landing on my feet but alas often on my backside. These were all perfectly reasonable athletic things to do and, along with running around the gym and doing circuit training, I enjoyed my gym periods to the full.

But when the teacher announced the picking of sides for basketball, my heart always sank. I loved almost all the sports and competed to the best of my limited ability in football, rugby, cricket, softball and volleyball, but I just couldn't get used to the rules and rhythm of bouncing a ball and throwing it up at a hoop with a net on it. Therefore, because I wasn't ever going to be any good at it, I basically didn't like the sport, and I was always being criticised for doing something wrong which cost my team points. So eventually I resolved to fix this and become a decent point scorer by practising at the hoop one lunch time a week. This was not a good decision.

One day when I was practising, I as usual overshot with my attempt and the ball sailed past the hoop and down, to wedge itself between two stacked benches and the wall. I walked round to retrieve the ball, stretched over to grab it and pulled it out from behind the heavy benches. Except that I dislodged the top bench as I did so. I leapt back to avoid the falling weight but it caught the big toe of my left foot. Ouch! Really Ouch! Gritting my teeth, I hobbled back to the changing room to assess the damage, but as soon as I took off my plimsoll I could see it wasn't good news. Blood was spreading out through my sock from my big toe and it wasn't stopping.

Someone alerted Mr. Chaplain who came in and carefully eased off my sock. Even he looked worried when we saw the toenail hanging half-off, and blood pouring from the flesh behind it. I felt dizzy at the sight of so much of my own blood. "Chappy" went to fetch a car and I was driven up to Dundee Royal Infirmary where he had to leave me at Accident & Emergency. I was very unhappy and a bit scared as I'd only ever been to hospital as a patient once before, to get stitches after I was knocked out by a swing during a game of Parachutes. The pain in my toe was excruciating and the blood was still oozing out as I was pushed along on a wheelchair to a treatment area. As I waited there, a big, burly nurse came along, crouched down for a closer look and then just pulled my nail completely off my toe with one yank! You could have heard me back at school.

Before I'd even stopped screaming she'd jabbed a hypodermic into my left thigh and then wandered off. When I looked back down at my big toe, the nail had gone and now there was a long gash across the bit where it had been. It was horrible to look at and it was bleeding profusely again. I was momentarily distracted by a younger nurse who got me onto a trolley and told me they'd have to stitch that gash. I suspected this was going to hurt, and when the first nurse who'd taken off my toenail came back with a tray full of evil-looking implements, I knew my fate was sealed.

The first stitch caused total agony and I couldn't hold back the tears any longer. I asked for some anaesthetic but the big nurse said to do that she'd have to stick the needle right in my toe where the gash was, so I'd probably be better without it. I agreed. The younger nurse offered to hold my hand, and I thought that was a very good idea, but she was ordered to do no such thing by her colleague, because I was too grown up for that. Oh really? The following three stitches were equally awful and I was completely overcome by the ordeal. I was repaired but traumatised. Once a bandage was applied, I was discharged and sent home.

To get there I had to hobble/shuffle/hop down through Dudhope Park on crutches which I couldn't work, to catch the 29 bus on Lochee Road. A kindly old lady asked why I was distressed. She gave me loads of sympathy and a sweet when I told her what had just happened. The walk up Craigowan Road to South Road was slow and very uncomfortable for me and it seemed to take forever to reach our close. I called up to the window for some help but of course no-one was in, so I was forced to crawl up four flights of stairs and let myself in. Joe came back first. He had heard at school I'd been taken away to the DRI so was very keen to get the whole story and examine my injured toe. He was very disappointed when he saw it was covered in a bandage and immediately lost interest. Mum and Dad gave me plenty of sympathy though and put me to bed where I was spoiled with treats for the next few days.

I think I was off school for about a week then went back on crutches for a couple of days after I'd had my stitches out. I dreaded having them taken out but that bit wasn't bad at all. I probably hated more the fact that my injury cost me about six weeks of football. That was indeed a terrible price to pay, adding insult to injury. Having stitches in hospital really was as awful an experience as I had imagined it would be, and the bad memory of my visit to the DRI took a great deal of time to evaporate.

And now you know why I don't like basketball.

23

Joe

In the run-up to Christmas 1966, it became clear that brother Joe wasn't exactly the "good wee laddie" the family thought him to be. He had by then enthusiastically embraced just about every sin available to him and, just when he was expected to knuckle down to his Highers after bagging 7 "O" Grades in fourth year, he launched into a spate of even greater misdemeanours. Had she known the whole truth, Mum would have been wringing her hands and praying to St. Jude, the patron saint of lost causes. I had to do my bit to keep him from getting rumbled but it was close at times and I knew one day he'd come unstuck.

Joe the prize-winner (front row, far right)

For a start he was getting a fair taste for the drink, not only at the weekends but during the week, especially at his pal Graeme's house up in Menzieshill. Although Graeme was a nice enough young man and a fairly close friend of both of us, I suspect that a major attraction of his flat was the inordinate amount of home brewed lager he seemed to always have there. Lots of lads of Joe's age were turning to home brew in an effort to get drunk as cheaply as possible and it was common knowledge that, even if it didn't always taste that great, it was guaranteed to get you legless with only three or four pints.

Luckily Graeme lived uphill from us otherwise Joe might not always have made it all the way back after a drinking session with him. Staggering downhill through the field, Joe required neither concentration nor navigation: he just set off at the top and eventually reached the old railway embankment between the field and South Road. From there it was just a matter of crossing the road without being run over and then heading for our tenement. He confided in me that climbing the four flights of stairs was sometimes a bit of a challenge, but not as difficult as focussing long enough to get the key in the door, turn it the right way and come in without attracting the attention of Mum or Dad.

Once in our bedroom, Joe would collapse on his bed, leaving his wee brother to put the blankets over him (often fully-dressed) and sneak a basin under his bed just in case. This pantomime was of course fraught with danger and Joe eventually adopted the tactic of staying over at his pal's house. If he did that, he could also have a cigarette or ten because by then his school blazer pocket was never without a packet of Number 6 in it. Nearly all of his pals smoked too, many even in the presence of their parents, but there was no chance of that happening at our house. When they visited, Joe's pals would be invited by my Mum and Dad to go downstairs and have a puff at the entrance to the close. Coming from two smokers as our parents were, that was a bit hypocritical, but rules were rules and ours was not to reason why.

Apart from his continuing deep interest in girls, Joe's other predilection was gambling at cards. We'd both developed a taste for card games from our parents, who found a Friday-night family game round the dining table was the perfect way to end the working week. That's why we knew how to play the commonest games like Trumps, Newmarket, Pontoon, Rummy and our very favourite, 9-Card Brag. The playing chips at home were always matches and they all went back into the Bluebell box at the end.

When we played with our friends there were two vital differences. Firstly, 9-Card Brag was replaced with the more exciting 3-card game, and second we played for money rather than matches. You had to stump up a penny to enter the game and then the pot either rose by a penny a round, or shot up as high as sixpence if luck had given somebody an especially good hand. As in poker, which we didn't then play, you had to add a final sum to the pot to see your opponent's hand. The game also allowed a player to bluff his way to victory if the others took cold feet and packed in their hands. On such occasions the victor would delight in returning his three cards to the pack without ever revealing what he'd had in his hand. The other players would never know if he'd bluffed or not.

A further edgy aspect of 3-Card Brag was the ability to play "blind" i.e. without even looking at your three cards. If anyone chose to play their hand this way the others had to put in double what the "blind" player added to the pot. Really good hands were often packed as the players were overcome with anxiety, but equally a mere pair or an ace high could reap a reward when the "blind" hand was turned over to reveal nothing of any value. Joe played "blind" a lot as he liked the thrill of this hazardous approach, but he emerged more often than not with more money than he'd started with.

Drink, fags, girls and gambling – you might imagine a sure-fire way of descending into the abyss and in many cases you'd be right. But we mustn't forget that Joe was clever, very clever, so he kept himself just far enough from the dark side to be able to shine as a senior pupil and have our parents think he was at the library with his pals on a Friday night.

Well, I suspect Mum and Dad didn't really believe that, but they said nothing and let him have his fun as long as he didn't get into any serious trouble.

Joe, letting me do the rowing!

However, Joe had a fifth vice. It was shooting. Now since our encounter with a gun-toting Crazy outside Camperdown Park about four years earlier, Joe had always wanted to have something to shoot with. He now owned two weapons. The smaller of the two was a spring-loaded .177 pistol which you primed by pushing in the extended inner barrel. When you pulled the trigger the inner barrel leapt forward and shot out the ammunition - either pellets or little darts with coloured feathers on them. It was with this pistol that I'd shot a dart into a holy picture on the window-sill when it was spooking me.

His other weapon was a much more powerful and therefore more dangerous .22 air rifle that he used for shooting birds or rabbits in Mains of Gray or Camperdown Park. I'd been allowed to try this rifle myself and I knew it could take down a sparrow at 50 yards, so it was by no means a toy. It's surprising how many of Joe's friends also had some kind of an air weapon, especially his eccentric friend Albin who appeared to have a whole collection of pistols and rifles. However, Joe's fun came to an end in the space of a few weeks and it cost him dear.

The first incident happened in Camperdown Woods when Joe and his pals chanced upon another group of boys with air guns, out doing the same thing as them. Typical pleasantries were exchanged, but one of the other group took things further and fired a pellet. Moments later there was an airgun fight going on, to the glee of both parties. However, someone else obviously thought it was very dangerous because the next thing the boys knew the woods seemed to be teeming with police and both groups were rounded up, the weapons confiscated and names taken. Joe luckily didn't have his rifle with him, and on seeing the police, had stuffed his pistol down the back of his pants. But an observant bobby spotted it and relieved him of the weapon in quite a robust manner.

One Sunday afternoon just a few weeks later, Joe and his friend Albin were returning from Mains of Gray where they'd hoped to bag a rabbit or two with their .22 air rifles. Fortunately for the rabbits they'd been unsuccessful and having stopped early, were coming back in broad daylight up the abandoned South Road railway line. Vitally they had both decided to keep their weapons unbagged in the hope of taking down some pigeons instead. It was a serious mistake to go wandering up the embankment when there were residential homes to their left and children out playing.

All at once there were police in front and behind, shouting at them to drop their weapons and stay still. Both boys did so immediately. Later, down in Bell Street police station, with weapons confiscated, the boys awaited the arrival of their parents who were informed that their sons were guilty of being in possession of loaded air rifles in a built-up area. Mum and Dad were horrified and Joe got the rollicking of his life. But a couple of days later, Albin and Joe had to appear individually before Dundee's strictest lawman, Sherriff Christie, who read them the riot act and more, issuing threats of time in the cells for any repeat of such dangerous conduct. Only clean criminal records and good school reports saved their bacon. And Joe never lifted another gun for several years. He did however buy some arrows from a sports shop and make himself a longbow!

Was Joe just being a typical wild working-class boy? I always thought that we were quite far down the social pecking-order because we didn't talk posh or have much money to spend on holidays and such. However, we were reasonably civilised and well educated, following Mum's plans for us to work hard and become something in the world. Our neighbours in 593 South Road were all very respectable and looked after the close, stairs and back green diligently. There wasn't much swearing or violence, some of us attended churches on Sunday, and noise was kept to a minimum except for celebrations. In truth we were doing alright and we believed that we'd never be left to sink if times got really hard.

Then the BBC Wednesday Play "Cathy Come Home" showed a young couple get married, have children, and fall on hard times when the husband could no longer work after an accident. Their downward spiral into homelessness was shocking to us all who trusted that our Welfare State would always be a safety net. Mum was howling by the end of the programme, distraught for Cathy as Social Services took her children away. This revelatory story made a huge impression on me and I realised that poor though we were, I was actually quite comfortably off in terms of the care I received, my education, family ties and the regular income from Dad's bus driving. We were clothed and fed: the play reminded me that not everyone in Britain might be so fortunate.

Joe and I had learned to make do. There were plenty of things we'd have liked to have, but it was drummed into us that clothes and food came first, followed by paying the rent and putting a shilling in the gas meter, then saving a few bob for the electricity, summer holiday and birthdays. Even the little money we put in the collection plate at Mass on Sunday was reckoned in the accounts, and all-in-all there wasn't an awful lot left over. But we were far from penniless and so we boys could still look forward to presents at Christmas and on Birthdays.

For Christmas of 1966 we had a joint present in mind – a record player. All our pals seemed to have one and we desperately wanted to invite them over to listen to records on our own turntable. The pop music scene was totally amazing at that time and we had a list of dozens of 45s we hoped to buy from Cathy McCabe's record store in the Arcade. I had top of my list two songs by Dave, Dee, Dozy, Beaky, Mick and Tich called *"Hold Tight"* and *"Bend it"* as well as a whole stack of Beatles hits. Joe's tastes were a bit more eclectic and he was impressed by the American four-part harmonies of The Beach Boys with their *"Good Vibrations"* and *"God Only Knows"*. So heading up our wish lists were that record player and the price of two singles each.

That Christmas Joe got a fountain pen and I got a pogo stick.

24

Choices

Not long after Christmas, the school began the process of getting us to choose the subjects we wanted to study for "O" Grades at the end of fourth year. This would shape our futures because our selections would determine the qualifications we'd leave school with. To start things off, we were given a printed sheet marked with column headers, underneath which were listed subjects it was possible to take as a group. Some subjects were listed in more than one column, so we had a fairly flexible choice.

We were told to go home and discuss this, because our Mums and Dads would attend the Parents' Night to meet the subject teachers and then at a later date talk to a House Head or the Headmaster himself. My folks took my education very, very seriously and we set aside an evening to work out what we'd say to the teachers. It was all very democratic. I was allowed to say exactly what I thought about each subject and why I might or might not want to continue with it. Mum chipped in with questions about implications for a future career while Dad made a lot of "when I was at school" comments. Hearing of his education in Twenties' Yorkshire, and tales of Technical teachers throwing wooden mallets at pupils, I really hoped things were going to be different for me.

We dealt with the easy stuff first. For 2A Boys, English and Maths were compulsory, as I think was French. I had to select History, Geography or a fairly new thing called Modern Studies in one column. I just plumped for the new one on the grounds that I didn't particularly enjoy History or Geography and some of my best pals were taking Modern Studies, although I omitted to tell my parents that. I admit that I gave rather an exaggerated description of the workload in the other two subjects, just to nudge Mum and Dad nearer agreement with me.

Bill must have blacked out during the game, unnoticed by the yelling crowd, for now he was alone in the vast stadium where, only an hour ago, thousands had been screaming for joy as the New York Yankees chalked up more "homers."

There was an eerie sense of tranquility in the air and the whole stadium seemed dead, the only sign of former life being the immense amount of litter which was strewn over the terracing. His first thought was of contriving a means of escape, so he walked towards the large railing-gates which were the main exits. As he passed under the covered enclosure, there was a flapping of wings and a pigeon scuttered out of its hiding place. Nervous as he was, he instinctively leapt the small barrier and darted onto the field but, as he reached the middle of the diamond, he had the strangest feeling that he was being watched—he came to a sudden halt.

Then, without reason, the floodlights flickered into life and pinpointed him in the centre of the arena. He gasped in terror and fled, as if the devil himself was at his heels, towards the small, metal turnstiles set in the concrete walls. But, unfortunately, he tripped over a stray cat which was stalking in the shadows and, as he lay still, he could hear footsteps, coming nearer. He pulled himself to his feet and continued his frenzied escape. "Hey," a voice echoed throughout the stadium—but the shock was too much for nervous Bill, and he slumped dead to the ground. The figure approached. "Gee; this one sure got all worked up about the Dodgers losing," it said, and the groundsman then entered the office and called the Morgue.   George Burton, 2A Boys.

Did I really write this?

A huge stumbling-block for an easy life at school over the next two years was the question of Science. Although it was 1967 and we were in the top class, none of the three Sciences was compulsory, so I had the option to completely get rid of the things I'd struggled with in the previous eighteen months. A life without Physics or Chemistry seemed highly attractive to me at that point. I knew it might be a hard case to argue with the teachers, though Mum and Dad offered little resistance to my appeals for relief.

The ace up my sleeve took the form of June Barclay, on whom I had a huge crush. Alternatives to Physics, Chemistry and Biology in one column were two other languages - Spanish and German. I knew already via a friend of a friend that the lovely June intended studying German the following year. With that uppermost in my thoughts I set out a plausible argument that I'd need to drop Science completely to be able to pursue my Latin and add a further foreign language to my French. I had decided to concentrate on Languages, and that would now include German. Mum and Dad were quite pleased with my mature decision, and congratulated me on being so sensible in my long-term approach to study. I sensed I had got away with it.

The seventh subject was Arithmetic, another compulsory one. This was basically counting and had none of the mind-boggling mysteries of

Geometry, Algebra and Trigonometry in it. Over two exams in first year and another two in second year, I'd managed not to drop a single mark and, along with a lot of my classmates, I considered Arithmetic "O" Grade as a bit of a gift. It was hard luck for the one or two of us who simply couldn't get the rules of counting into their heads. Those questions about filling the bathtub with water while stupidly leaving the plug out, and gangs of men digging ditches non-stop for days, struck fear into their hearts.

Discussion of my options turned out quite successfully, and even Joe took the time to pop his head round the living-room door to add his support for my choices. So Mum filled in the form and signed it. Hooray! Stage One of my plan was complete. But Stage Two was a different matter, especially when our appointment card showed that my parents and I would be discussing my choices with Mr. Adams, the Headmaster. This man seemed to know everything about all of the pupils at Lawside, both their studies and their families. Pulling any wool over his experienced eyes would be much more difficult than it had been with my parents.

Yet the Parents' Night passed without a problem. The teachers whose subjects I'd chosen seemed fairly happy that I was going to be in their classes, while those whose subjects I intended to no longer study were not unhappy to lose me. The exception

211

was Mr. Mulligan the History Teacher, who insisted that History was the subject for all the cleverest people. You could see that in the teams who took part in *University Challenge* on TV. I was very grateful that he didn't push his case too hard and I didn't have to change my choice. The Art and Music teachers 'thanked me for my efforts' and Mr. Miller even said my drawings of horses' heads weren't too bad. So there was only the final Interview to come.

Meanwhile, out in the playgrounds, there was a lot of discussion about who was taking what. Even for the most able pupils, the most important factor in these decisions appeared to be which friends were going to share the class with you. Hardly anyone was taking a subject where the teacher had been particularly nasty in the previous two years, even if the subject itself was interesting and useful. On the other hand, some not-so-riveting subjects did benefit from the popularity of the teachers who taught them.

I kept quiet as to what made me choose German instead of Science, but I was happy that I would be in the same classroom as June Barclay for the next two years. I wouldn't have cared if she'd opted for Domestic Science instead of German! I figured that being in that German class would give me opportunities to impress her with my brains and wit, even if I might not yet have impressed her with my looks. I had noticed how the best-looking boys had the pick of the crop, but also how some boys' success quite clearly depended on their charm and patter. That's the way I intended to go.

At about Easter time, my folks and I attended the school Careers Evening, where we met representatives from all the professions and the Forces, as well as local firms who were looking for the best apprentices. I was particularly impressed by a couple of Insurance companies who described exciting work both indoors and out, dealing with dynamic situations like fires, air crashes and earthquakes. That sounded like fun. My Yorkshire Auntie Pat had recently married Brian, who worked for an Insurance company, and he'd told me it was interesting work. So I left with a few new ideas.

The day of our Interview with the Headmaster arrived. I was very nervous when we went into Mr. Adams' room but I needn't have been as he was to the point and emphatic in his assessment of my potential. I was quite clever, particularly strong in Maths, and capable with Languages both Classical and Modern, so it was obvious that I'd turn out to be .... an actuary! My course choices met with his approval and he expected me to pass all seven of my "O" Grades and then get five good Highers. Thereafter, following a sixth year at Lawside I should continue to University to study Maths then join a firm and become an actuary. Thank you and goodnight.

The first thing we did when we got home was get out the Encyclopaedia Britannica and look up "actuary" to see what Mr. Adams thought I should be. None of us knew what an actuary did. It turned out they were the people in Life Assurance who worked out the life expectancy of customers in order to calculate how big the premium should be and how big a risk the company would run. That didn't sound too bad, and it was in Insurance as well. We decided to go with it and I slept soundly that night, happy in the knowledge that I was going to be a successful actuary, even if not very many people knew what that was.

The final episode in my Choices saga was checking that June Barclay hadn't changed her mind at the last moment about taking German. Again, via a friend of a friend, I tried to find out. I was agitated to discover that she hadn't yet had her interview. It was with Sister Mary Agnes, and I was filled with dread that she might be persuaded to become a nun in a Closed Order. Two or three uncomfortable days later I got the news I'd been hoping for. After two years in all-male classes, Georgie Burton was going to be sitting next to (well, at worst not too far away from) the beautiful girl he was in love with. My life would be complete!

25

Football

The spring and early summer of 1967 was so good for our football that at times we didn't quite believe it ourselves, though we had already had our eyes opened at that amazing double victory of Dundee United over Barcelona before the turn of the year. I was a staunch dark-blue supporter, but I celebrated that incredible success as if my favourite team had done it themselves. It was like that in Dundee: there was rivalry but no insanity of the sort that characterised some supporters of Celtic and Rangers.

The next result to set others back on their heels came in mid-April when Scotland travelled down to Wembley to take on the English World Champions, still undefeated since the previous July when they'd lifted the Jules Rimet Trophy. It wasn't the fact that the Scots won 3-2 which caused a stir, but it was the manner of the victory over the Auld Enemy, a display of outrageous arrogance that left jaws gaping. For the following weeks we would all be in the playgrounds or over in the field trying to copy Slim Jim Baxter's *"keepie-uppie"* routine.

By the time that game took place, there was a real buzz around the grounds, with Celtic in the European Cup, Rangers in the Cup-Winners Cup and Kilmarnock in the Fairs Cities Cup. This was an unforeseen run of success for the Scottish clubs and, as Kilmarnock were eventually beaten by the great Leeds United, it was left to the two huge Glasgow clubs to carry the fight. Both succeeded in reaching their respective finals, and suddenly we were facing the wonderful possibility of both the major European trophies coming back to Scotland.

On 25 May 1967, with club allegiance temporarily put on hold, I sat huddled in front of the TV cheering on Celtic to victory over Inter Milan in Lisbon. The dream came true and a 2-1 victory for the Scots was hailed as the triumph of good old attacking football over the much-loathed *cattenacio* Italian defence. The country went crazy with delight and Celtic's manager, Jock Stein, was told by Liverpool's legendary Bill Shankley that he was now an Immortal.

Six days later, the other Glasgow club tried to emulate their great rivals, in the final of the European Cup-Winners Cup against the formidable Bayern Munich. This German team contained many players from their National side. Rangers, having scraped through their deadlocked quarter-final against Real Zaragoza on the mere toss of a coin, played their hearts out, but unluckily fell to an extra-time goal for the Germans.

With such startling events going on at professional level it was no wonder that many of us 14-year old boys spent every spare moment kicking a ball around, be it a tennis ball in the close, a plastic ball on the road and in the playground, a solid and dangerous Mitre ball or even an antique leather tube with inflatable nozzle tucked not-so-neatly under the lethal lace. If you caught that lace wrong with a header, it could split your scalp. Nothing was allowed to stop your daily game of football, not even lack of a ball. One of my friends and I had a perfectly reasonable game of headers in the washing green using a ball of mum's wool, and the football mania continued even in the house where Joe and I would enjoy a game in the long lobby using a balloon.

My Dad played quite a lot of football over in the field with us although he was coming up for fifty, because he had kept himself quite fit and active. He was joined by other Dads from the closes around us and once the game was over they would have a quick wash then stroll down to the Gaiety Bar for a pint. We boys got refreshment from the Bon-Accord lemonade lorry that came around the scheme every week, offering us exotic flavoured drinks like Limeade, Raspberryade, Pineappleade and American Cream Soda. Their Pola-Cola wasn't bad either.

The lemonade lorry

With all the football I was playing, I expected to begin to carve out a place in the Lawside football team for my age group. But I was going to be sorely disappointed, even though I wasn't a bad wee player and could double-up nicely as the goalkeeper. Sadly for us, there were many half-decent aspiring team players who like me were unfortunate enough to be in the same year-group as some of the finest young Lawside footballers ever to grace a school pitch. All eleven of our team were "S" signings linked to one or other of the Professional teams. This left us with little or no chance of being noticed by Mr. Hart, who ran the side and knew exactly what talent he had on his hands. This team won pretty much everything that school year and in the following season topped things off by becoming under-15 Scottish Shield winners. It was brilliant that my classmates were national champions but it still hurt a little that I couldn't get noticed.

Two great teams, under14s and under 15s

So, where did my brother Joe fit in to all of this? Truth to tell, he didn't. Other than becoming a Dundee United supporter for a few years and that probably just to wind up Dad and me, Joe never really committed himself to football or any other sport. He joined in to make the sides up and so on but though he was pretty good it was never his first choice of how to amuse himself of an evening, preferring to lie on his bed reading or to learn new songs on the guitar. I treated my brother with great respect, thinking of him as the intellectual of the family, a dreamer and philosopher. I was clever and doing well at school but he was a whole stage above me in smart thinking and the application of ideas. Where I was a bit of a copier, Joe was an inventor.

An example of this was what we'd do with the guitar. My endeavours with this instrument involved learning chords to accompany the words I'd sing, and trying to sound just a wee bit like the artists I was copying. Joe was a good mimic when it came to doing that but he had already moved on to making up his own tunes and his own lyrics, outdistancing me in the family musicianship stakes. Indeed it didn't even cross my mind to go down that road. My thoughts were elsewhere, burning with ambition to excel in physical sports despite my skinny body. I trained and practised football most days, and ever so gradually Georgie began to develop both in skill and in confidence.

The Scottish Shield-winning team

26

Check!

I turned fourteen on 17 February 1967 and once again I didn't get the record player I had wished for. In its place I got a different present and frankly one that changed my life. It was a chess set. It wasn't even a proper chess set with pieces and a board. It came in a box about the size of a slice of Mother's Pride bread and each chess piece had a little peg on the base that could fit into the hole in each square. So it was a portable chess set I suppose, the sort of thing you got at a jumble sale and probably an old present that somebody didn't want. That was a coincidence, as I didn't want it either.

Inevitably it was Joe who came to the rescue, no doubt feeling sorry for me and fed up of the long face I was wearing. At some point that evening he called me through to our bedroom, told me for God's sake to cheer up and said he was going to teach me how to play chess. I wasn't completely over the moon about this idea but dear brother persisted, and within an hour my bishops were flying diagonally across the board, my horses were leaping L-shaped hither and thither and my queen was running around like a headless chicken! Joe even taught me the four-move Scholar's Mate, but only after he'd used it on me about ten times.

Scholar's Mate

On the next convenient school lunchtime I enrolled myself in the Chess Club, overseen up in his lab by Mr. Price, a Science teacher. There were real chess sets there that I could play with, all Staunton pieces kept in little wooden boxes with sliding lids, and the boards were over a foot square and folded in the middle for storing. This was more like it, especially playing with one particular set whose chessmen had sand or something in their bases to make them heavy. Moving these weightier pieces around made the game feel very serious and made me think carefully about where I was going to put them. That very first lunchtime at Lawside Chess Club I lost every game except one (an agreed draw against a first year when the bell rang) but I had discovered a game I really liked, not as much as football of course, but still really liked.

222

From then on, for the next few weeks, I nagged and nagged at Joe to play chess with me in the bedroom at night. Being a sometimes indulgent brother, he actually spent quite a lot of time with me, explaining how to fork, pin, check, double-check, sacrifice and castle to keep the King safe. He introduced me to standard beginning moves called Openings, which would be very useful and stop me from losing quite so quickly, if I could be bothered to learn them. He also showed me that there was a code attached to each move that you could write down so you could replay a game in your own time and maybe see what you'd done wrong. How brilliant was that!

Helped by this code system I went about learning the main openings like the *Giuoco Piano* and the *Ruy Lopez*. It was a massive learning curve that took up an awful lot of my free time but it improved my ability dramatically. I think my natural swottishness helped me a lot, as I was happy to sit from after tea until bed time going over and over previously-played games. On the advice of Mr. Price I'd gone searching in the library for books on chess and I'd been surprised by the number of books filled with the games of past World Champions. I came across many exotic names like Capablanca, Morphy, Botvinnick, Tal, and Petrosian. I wondered why the Russians were so dominant in the upper ranks of world chess and then I discovered that their kids even got to play chess *as a school subject*. I was so envious of them.

223

But just four months later Georgie Burton was playing a Grand Master!

This remarkable turn of events resulted from my over-the-top enthusiasm and dedication to the school Chess Club, which I visited on many lunch times but always when it was raining: well, I wasn't stupid, was I? I helped set out the boards, tidied up when the bell rang and so on, and Mr. Price saw that I was serious about the game. He told me that towards the middle of July there was to be a Professional Grand Master tournament in Dundee, and the organisers needed young chess enthusiasts to control the giant display boards next to each table. Computers, videos and projection equipment weren't available for these purposes in the Dundee of 1967, so these boards, viewed from a respectable distance, allowed the general public to follow what was happening in each game (in total silence of course). I volunteered at once, and when I got home from school I had to anxiously enquire if we were going away on holiday in July. When Mum said we were going to be staying in Scotland this year, I had to explain why I was so delighted to hear that.

When I went to the training days in the Marryat Hall, attached to the even more splendid Caird Hall, all the important etiquette of attending a Grand Master tournament was explained. I had to practise unhooking the correct piece from the huge wooden display board and then snagging it back on in the position to which it had been moved, ensuring the pieces were securely hooked on to the L-shaped nails in the display board. Letting one crash to the ground was not recommended as a way of extending your stay when the three-day tournament was in progress.

On 11 July this Chess Grand Master Tournament began, celebrating the centenary of a previous such competition in Dundee, and there was Georgie Burton at one of the display boards, quietly moving the pieces around as soon as the players moved them on their actual chessboard. I knew some of the players there from reading about them in books. Bent Larsen was one of the world's best players at the time, Gligoric was a candidate for the World Championship Title, and Jonathan Penrose had been British Champion loads of times. There were two Scots playing as well, although I think they were a bit outclassed by the opposition. The player who fascinated me the most was a Belgian Grand Master who went by the astounding name of O'Kelly de Galway!

The highly-fancied Gligoric won the tournament by a full point and deservedly so. But the highlight for me came at the end of Day 3 when I was tidying things up. Bent Larsen from Denmark, who was soon to play against Russia on Board 1 for the Rest of the World while the legendary Bobby Fischer was only on Board 2, was sitting analysing an earlier win. As I passed his table he looked up and asked me very nicely if I'd like a game. I nearly fell over with excitement!

Grandmaster Bent Larsen with display board behind

He was polite and kind all the way through ten whole minutes of pawn-pushing and he was generous in victory over me, calling Mate then inviting me to double-check that he'd got it right. When I agreed that he did have me in checkmate, he gave a huge grin from below his great bushy eyebrows and shook my hand. What a moment that was for a chess beginner like me.

This experience sealed it for me and I set my sights on becoming a chess Grand Master. I played a lot and I played pretty well at various levels over the years. Despite trying hard, I never came close to achieving that status. But during my time as a player I made a friend called Paul Motwani. Paul became Scotland's first ever Grand Master.

I played in the school chess team right through until I left and encouraged many of my classmates to "take up the pawns". We ended up with more than one strong Lawside team playing in the Schools' Leagues and indeed won several trophies. Some of us played for Dundee Schools against Aberdeen etc. and we did well in the Sunday Times British Championships and the Scotsman Trophy although we never quite managed a final. I once just needed a draw to win the Dundee Easter Congress at my grade but plucked defeat from the jaws of victory, something I did repeatedly in all sorts of competitions, whether chess or not.

Thursday, February 11, 1971.

Lawside boys'
chess win

A team from Lawside Academy, Dundee, beat a team from Inverness Royal Academy by three games to one in a chess tournament at the Aviemore Centre yesterday, and are now in the quarter finals of the Scotsman Trophy.

The boys, accompanied by Mr John Price, chemistry master, 15 Brigend Street, were George Burton, David Jackson Tony Berrie and Peter McLaren.

One of our best results

27

St Andrews

As things turned out, I did still get a holiday during the summer of 1967 despite helping out at the Dundee chess tournament in the Marryat Hall. When the Dundee Holiday Fortnight came round, we took the train to St. Andrews and dragged our luggage past the East Sands and up the hill to the caravan site at Kinkell Braes. It was the third time we'd been there, as it had proved a good alternative to the Red Lion or Elliot Junction caravan parks in Arbroath. After all, there were only so many Smokies you could eat. St. Andrews was just about the same distance away as Arbroath, except that we headed south into the Kingdom of Fife.

Our site was perched on the edge of a cliff overlooking the second of St. Andrews' beaches. The West Sands were more famous as they ran alongside the Old Course. The massive reputation of this course among the world's golfers ensured that the little Fife town was always packed full of Americans fulfilling their dreams of playing a round at the Home of Golf. Luckily for us, the Open was being held in Liverpool that summer, otherwise I doubt if there would have been room in St. Andrews for the Burtons. But there we were, the four of us, in a little caravan near the middle of the site, surrounded by like-minded holidaymakers. We only had a few bob in our pockets but we were all determined to have a great time away from our normal surroundings.

We never went further away for holidays, except to visit the family in Leeds, because exotic sounding places like Great Yarmouth or Blackpool were outside the means of Mum and Dad. Anyway, they'd been told that Blackpool was always full of Glaswegians in the summer and those west coasters were usually regarded as a bit wild by us Dundonians. Foreign holidays weren't even considered. It was something that other people did, not us, nor indeed any of our friends and relations. Even if we'd had the money, there would have been no chance of Mum boarding an aeroplane. She wasn't terribly keen on getting higher off the ground than was absolutely necessary.

That's why Mum didn't really enjoy our first adventure the day after we arrived to stay at Kinkell Braes, because Joe and I insisted on going up St. Rule's Tower, standing within the ruins of St. Andrews' 800 year-old Cathedral. We were thrilled to climb the hundred foot tower and emerge on to a platform. It was about ten feet square and had a wall that only came up to waist height, with a built-in seat all the way round. Mum and Dad had come up with us, probably to prevent us from doing anything stupid once we were up there, and to be fair they'd managed the spiral staircase without much of a problem.

But once she came out at the top into the clear light of day, it immediately became obvious that this wasn't our dear mother's preferred spot from which to enjoy the historic sights of St. Andrews. As Joe and I posed like human flies for photos near the edge of the dizzying drop, Mum tried her best to keep her eyes on us without actually opening them. She was very, very happy when Dad made us start back down, despite our pleas for one more lean out over the edge. On our way back to the caravan, Mum's ever-fragile nerves got the better of her and Dad took her into an East Sands pub for a quick calming drink just before closing time at half past two. Mum's new favourite tipple was OVD rum and coke, which had superseded a lifetime commitment to Advocaat and lemonade.

At the top of St. Rule's Tower

That pub shone an interesting light on the biblical Commandment *"Thou shalt not steal"*. You see, the Burtons didn't steal. Well, not habitually anyway. Admittedly Joe and I had crawled through the back greens when we were younger and eaten rhubarb or carrots straight from the ground in our neighbours' plots, but that didn't really seem like a sin, even if it had been the major admission to the priest at my First Confession. Joe might have liberated the odd Woodbine from Mum's packet on the mantelpiece, but taking something like that from a parent again didn't seem to fit the bill. Even Mum had maximised the amount of bedroom damage caused by an intruding firework, but that surely wasn't so bad either, not compared with my mate Walter robbing shops blind all the way through Primary School. No, we didn't take other people's property. Or did we?

After tea, the early evenings at Kinkell Braes were spent having adventures at the beach, in the rock pools or on the cliffs, especially the giant pinnacle which graced the shoreline a couple of hundred yards from the caravan site. There was enough entertainment in these areas to keep us occupied for hours. Meanwhile Mum and Dad would go down to that pub at the East Sands not a quarter of a mile away and have a couple of drinks, while Mum fed her holiday money into whatever fruit machine happened to be on the premises. Joe and I, at 16 and 14 respectively, weren't allowed into pubs even for a lemonade, so there was no question of us being with our parents if they wanted a holiday snifter or two. Ours were by no means the only parents who did this and we met many kids clambering over the rocks whose parents were probably in the same pub as Mum and Dad.

So when they came back to the caravan at about half past ten on the last night of our stay, lit the gas mantles and got out the cards, Joe and I took our places at the foldaway table, ready to rake in as many matches as we could win. Mum sorted us boys out with a glass of Creamola Foam, Dad took his little can-opener and punched two holes in his Tennant's Lager tin and Mum sat down with what was left of her holiday half bottle of OVD rum and the remains of a bottle of Pola-Cola she'd bought. And she mixed her drink in a glass we hadn't seen before.

This was odd. I asked Mum where that glass had come from and she blushed a little bit. Then she admitted that she'd taken it from the pub, because she'd only just started her last drink when closing time was called and she would've had to leave a nearly-full glass of rum on the table when invited to exit the premises by the barman. She couldn't drink it right down but she couldn't bring herself to let the rum go to waste. She would say no more. I helpfully expressed my view that she'd probably go to hell for that.

The fact that she'd taken something that didn't belong to her must have been weighing on Mum's mind, because one Friday night when we were all back in Dundee, I heard her tell Dad that she had confessed her misdemeanour to the priest at St. Clements' church. To her shame and shock the priest had told her the sin would be forgiven once the stolen item was returned to the rightful owner. And true to her personal faith, Mum made Dad take her all the way back to St. Andrews on the train and along to that pub, just so she could go in, order a drink and quietly sneak that glass out of her handbag and onto the table. They drank up, left, and got back on the train. Mum felt hugely relieved and no doubt thought that she now had a better chance of getting to heaven.

Mum, me and Joe at the castle pool

Joe and I spent most of that holiday at the town end of the East Sands, playing putting, fishing at the harbour, or swimming in the sea. There was also an old disused swimming pool at the foot of the castle that was still very popular with the holidaymakers. Joe and I would have a swim there now and again, or, from the tiny beach in front of it, we could also reach the slanting black rocks at the water's edge. Then we could make our way round the bottom of the cliff to the harbour wall. Halfway along, there was a cave in the cliff face to which we could climb up. Caves were always full of possibilities at my age.

Swimming was also possible (but not particularly comfortable) at the Step Rock pool just a short distance from the Royal & Ancient Clubhouse. This pool was fed twice a day by the tide of the North Sea and consequently was always breathtakingly freezing, especially when the wind was blowing. That was more or less every day in St. Andrews. The water was also much deeper than in the swimming baths we frequented in Dundee and, although Joe revelled in its challenge, I, being a considerably weaker swimmer than him, found the whole thing a bit scary. So I tended to be found clinging to the side of the pool more often than actually swimming from one side to the other. The seaweed wrapping itself around my legs didn't make me feel any more confident either!

Step Rock Pool (Used by kind permission of DC Thomson & Co Ltd)

But fishing was always the highlight of the holiday and very popular with Mum and Dad because it kept us busy and away from under their feet for many hours at a time. It also cost them almost nothing. Where the Kinness Burn met the sea, there was a lock topped by a footbridge that could be opened for smaller boats when they arrived at the harbour. This little bridge linked the East Sands to the Castle cliffs and the high main pier, which we loved to walk along as if we were red-gowned students. The torchlight pier walk was a University tradition, but ordinary folk walked the pier too. It was completely exposed high above the rocks, and there was no protection on either side of the uneven surface you stepped on. Our whole family did it many times, but Mum of course often found something less perilous to do.

Fishing with our orange sea lines was one option at the little bridge but, as the water wasn't very deep except at high tide, we just used a simple line of catgut with a small hook at the end and a float with lead sinkers. We liked to sit on top of the lock gate, out of sight below the wooden walkway where the holidaymakers would cross. Flounders were our main bounty, tiddlers and crabs abounded, but we all wanted to catch a sea trout. To my amazement Joe did just that one day, hauling the hapless fish up onto the top of the lock gate where we were stationed for the day. In these rather cramped conditions, Joe managed to wind in the fish, knock it out and unhook it. He proudly laid it down between us. I asked for permission to hold it, then picked it up carefully and stared straight into its eyes. It looked at me blankly. And then it twitched. Startled, I let go, there was a splash and it was gone. My brother was less than delighted at what had happened and it would be fair to say that I nearly accompanied that sea trout into St. Andrews harbour and the North Sea beyond.

One final delight for holidaymakers at St. Andrews was the walk on the Old Course on Sunday morning as, despite its worldwide reputation, the Links course was shut on the Sabbath. In my mind all the Sundays we were there seemed to be crowned with beautiful weather and we were happy to join lots of other people strolling around the most famous golf course in the world.

Joe and me on the West Sands

Of course, we'd keep off the huge double-greens, but sometimes the temptation of a roll down the sand of the redoubtable Hell Bunker was more than I could resist. Joe and I would usually compete to see who could jump the Swilken Burn at its widest points, and surprisingly neither of us ever ended up in the water protecting the first green.

28

Romance

At Lawside Academy in August 1967, the main focus of my third year was the German class because that's where June Barclay was. I simply couldn't wait to get into Slip Mahoney's German lessons just so I could sit close to the girl I had fallen in love with. She didn't know I was in love with her (or if she did she seemed to act really cool about it) and I knew that at least I was going to have to speak to her before going so far as to ask her out. Hopefully my first face-to-face conversation with her wouldn't be totally educational, like asking her in German for directions to the train station.

We boys had of course been becoming more curious about females over a few years and we were endlessly seeking information to fill the gaps in our knowledge. There was a paper called "Reveille" that my Uncle Stan got, which was fairly boring but always contained an array of bikini-clad beauties. These girls were covered up in all the wrong places as far as I was concerned but they did suggest there was something worth seeing underneath. It was a pity I wasn't quite sure what. One of my pals once smuggled an old Pirelli calendar from the garage his Dad worked in and those topless photos did the rounds for a while but, with the TV having a complete 'No Nudity' policy, there wasn't actually much chance of me seeing a lot of what we were all desperate to see.

It was also very similar at the cinema as far as nudity went, with the exception of Dundee's Tivoli where it was reported you could see all sorts of things on the foreign films they showed there. Still, we were too young to have a chance of getting in and the place itself had a pretty bad reputation for 'old men in raincoats'. I didn't really understand what people meant when they said that. On one memorable occasion in Coupar Angus, Peter and Joe said they were going to the local cinema that evening to see a Brigitte Bardot film and they casually told me that naturally she would be stripping off at some point in the plot. How I begged them to let me go with them. They eventually accepted but only on the basis they wouldn't defend me if I was refused admittance, because it was an "X" certificate. They were seventeen and sixteen respectively and would have no problem getting in, especially with Pete's mate on the door, but admitting someone of my age might be another matter entirely.

As I waited in the queue, I couldn't take my eyes off the poster outside that showed a scantily-clad Brigitte helpless in the clutches of an armed desperado. "Please not now" said the caption, and to my overheating imagination it was obvious she'd be forced by her captor to reveal all. I was only just able to concentrate on squeezing close up between my brother and my big cousin as we reached the door, hiding my fresh face as much as I could, but wonder of wonders the ploy was successful and I got in. There then followed 80 minutes of complete boredom until the heroine found herself alone in a room with the man with the gun. He told her to take her clothes off, all of them!

A naked shoulder here, long legs there and suddenly she was naked ... with her back to the camera. Oh no! But then the man with the gun told her to turn round. This was it. She turned, and the camera zoomed in on the upper half of her body. Yes! No! She had her arms crossed just where I didn't want her to. Then to my delight he told her to put her arms by her side. Good idea! She started to obey him. Here it was then, the big moment. Brigitte Bardot revealed! But as her arms fell to her sides, that blasted camera zoomed in further to a point just above the middle of her chest. My hopes were dashed! I barely noticed her on-screen boyfriend crash through the door and shoot her captor, saving the day. He gave Brigitte a coat to put on and the movie was over. The three of us left the cinema disappointed but, although Joe and Peter laughed it off, I was disgusted with the sneakiness of the film makers and I decided that one day I'd be going to the Tivoli to see the real thing on screen. But to be honest, I never got round to it.

Another source of excitement was to go to one of Dundee's second-hand bookshops where it was reputed they kept 'dirty' books. There was one on the corner of Bank Street in Lochee, just where South Road began, and in my innocence I had been walking past it for years, without even looking at the books in the window. On several later occasions I resolved to go in but I always lost my nerve once I eventually forced myself through the door, and ended up with a Commando magazine I'd probably already read.

The nearest I came to getting a spicy book there was the time I planned to go in and tell the shop owner that my cousin Tony was back on leave from the RAF and was very tired so had asked me to go to the bookshop and get him a copy of *"Peyton Place"*. Hugely popular on TV, this novel by Grace Metalious was rumoured to have wildly graphic 'dirty' bits in it so that explained my choice. For once, my curiosity overcame my timidity and I marched in confidently and boldly. Except that the man behind the counter saw through my foolproof scheme in an instant and asked me to tell my poor tired cousin to pop in himself once he'd had a good night's sleep!

I began to think I would never ever get the chance to see what everybody else seemed to know about in detail, even those the same age as me. Their stories were all made up of course, but somehow I usually believed them, assuming it was just me that was ignorant of that side of life. Things would change soon enough of course but that was to come.

So getting back to my infatuation with June Barclay, I discussed the matter with my new pal, that sexual sophisticate Charlie Maclean. I still knocked around with Dougie, Phillip and the very unusual Jay, but Charlie and I had somehow gravitated towards each other and we were by now officially best friends. Charlie was undeniably having more luck than me with the opposite sex, so I valued his opinion and advice. He told me that attracting girls was all about smiling, saying smart things and being "cool" but above all, about making them laugh. Without hesitation I started to practice saying funny things, hoping I'd be able to come out with one or two good lines when an opportunity arose.

Just as visiting Phillip had been risky, there was a problem in that Charlie lived on the other side of town in an area of Linlathen called Honeygreen. That had the potential to make life difficult for a Charleston boy now that Dundee was inhabited by several teenage gangs with their own territories and uniforms. We got round this by never mentioning where I came from when I visited the Maclean home, especially if we went out for chips or decided to cross the Fintry Bridge.

This bridge, an old aqueduct dating back to the nineteenth century, crossed a low-lying area where the Dighty Burn made its way to the sea at Monifieth. It was about 500 feet long and stood between the Fintry and Linlathen housing estates, with some arches rising over twenty feet above the meadows below. So, once you were on the bridge itself, you'd hurry to get to the other end in case a group of boys suddenly appeared. Charlie was safe being a local but there was no guarantee I would be left alone. The one time things looked dicey, I jumped off a lower part of the bridge and ran for the safety of the Forfar Road.

Dighty Bridge (used with the kind permission of D C Thompson Ltd)

It was a bit easier when Charlie came down to visit me as we didn't really have much of a gang issue. Lots of kids thought Charleston boys would be in the dreaded Lochee Fleet, one of the biggest gangs

243

in the town. We weren't, but we did know a few individual gang boys quite well, which was very useful in health terms if we ran into a group of them when they were looking for trouble. So Charlie spent a good deal of time with me down on South Road, playing football in the field or roving the streets checking out the girls. I also introduced Charlie to chess, my own passion of that time, and we often found ourselves hiding away in my bedroom swopping pawns, especially if the weather was bad. In fact Charlie became good enough to get into one of the school teams and even made the Dundee Select team at one point.

When Christmas arrived, Joe and I finally got the record-player we'd been requesting for 2 years. Now that would help to impress the ladies! We couldn't wait to play a record on it of course, but with the shops closed for a few days it was into the New Year before we got down to Cathy McCabe's record shop to make our choice. Well, what was it going to be? Obviously *"Hello, Goodbye"* by the Beatles was tempting at number 1 but there were dozens of great songs out at that time. We'd been listening eagerly to the new BBC Radio 1 since its launch in September, so we knew most of them quite well. The Burton brothers could do a fair rendering on guitar and vocals of Georgie Fame's *"Ballad of Bonnie and Clyde"* and we were also working on The Monkees' *"Daydream Believer"*. I said we should get a new record *"Everlasting Love"* by Love Affair, but typically Joe and I ended up buying none of them and eventually plumped for *"Baby Now That I've Found You"* by the Foundations.

Next pocket money day we added *"The Mighty Quinn"* by Manfred Mann and we played these two 45s to death. Generally our musical tastes were quite similar and the quarrelling was kept to a minimum.

So, did that help with June Barclay? Well, I'd been doing my best to impress her with my wit in German class as well as making sure I was top of that class. She seemed to like my taste in music and the things I'd say, and she did laugh at them, but she wasn't always turning round to stare at me during the class. So I came up with another idea. I'd ask someone else out.

That's not as bad as it sounds because I liked the girl I intended to ask out and she was probably second on my list of desirables. Her name was Janice Orr and she had a relative in Coupar Angus, so I'd already talked to her both in and out of school. Charlie agreed it was about time I went out on a date, but he thought I should just ask June. I had to confess that I didn't have the nerve yet, but I asked him to help me approach Janice on Friday at lunchtime.

That's why we found ourselves doing clockwise lap after lap of the internal quadrangle, while Janice and her pals walked anti-clockwise, giving me lots of opportunities to ask her out. After about an hour, with lunchtime coming to an end I finally summoned up the courage. But she forthwith disappeared into the main playground and suddenly the school bell was ringing.

Lining up in the main playground

Charlie couldn't stop laughing. I thought all was lost but at that moment Janice and two friends came back round the corner and I surprised both Charlie and myself by walking straight over to her and saying "Hi, Janice". As if by magic, her friends turned back the way they'd come. I just blurted out that I'd like her to come to the cinema with me. She said yes almost before I'd finished the question. We agreed to meet below Samuel's clock in the Nethergate on Saturday night at seven o'clock. When I turned to Charlie, he could see it had gone well, so he came over and shook my hand. I had just successfully arranged my first date.

Samuel's Corner (used with the kind permission of D C Thompson Ltd)

For the record, Janice turned up on time and we went to Green's Playhouse where I spent a month's pocket money to pay us into the Golden Divans. We saw the newly-released musical *"Camelot"* starring Richard Harris; I bought her a choc-ice and a carton of Kia-Ora at the interval. She said she'd had a great time and she kissed me just before she got on the bus home.

That left it open for me to ask her out again. For some reason I didn't and that was a big mistake because a couple of weeks later, at the end of the German class, I asked June out.

She said no.

And while lads of my age were distracted with thoughts of love and sex, something very evil walked our way. On the first of November, former St. John's High School pupil and army recruit Robert Mone walked into his old school just up the road from us. He was armed with a shotgun, and took a sewing class hostage. An hour and a half later he had abused some of the girls in the class and shot dead the pregnant teacher Mrs. Hanson. Many of my former pals from Primary School were in St. John's that day, including my old pal Eddie Weir. The attack on the innocent teacher and her pupils was international news and the eyes of the world fixed for a while on that Dundee secondary school.

Most of us couldn't believe it. It didn't seem possible that someone could get a shotgun, walk into their old school and kill a teacher for no apparent reason. It couldn't happen, not in Dundee anyway. And yet it just had. During the next few days it felt like there was nothing else to talk about, neither among my friends, on the TV nor in the papers. While lessons continued at Lawside, neither the teachers nor the pupils were concentrating anymore. For a while, any unexpected loud noise made us all jump and wait for something terrible to happen. Of course nothing did, but Robert Mone's actions affected us all and Dundee would never again feel quite as safe as it had been before.

29

Meter

When I was a wee boy I always looked forward to the gas meter being emptied, a bit like other kids looked forward to birthdays. My reason for this excitement was the rebate that Mum was given after the box of coins was removed. The gas man would check the number of units used, calculate how much was due to cover that much consumption, take that sum of money out of the box and leave the remainder on the table. As I ran the silver through my fingers I felt like a pirate in the olden days when he dug up treasure. To be honest it was a relatively small amount left by the man in the cap with the clipboard and torch, but because it was all in shilling coins, to my eyes it became riches beyond the dreams of wickedness.

Mum and I had fun counting the booty, piling and stacking the shillings this way and that, making patterns on the dining-table out of the silver coins and inevitably rolling them across the polished surface on their edges. Quite often a game of "shove-shilling" developed between us, a step up from "shove- ha'penny. It was a great pity that the electricity wasn't prepaid as well, or we could have had this excitement twice as often. There was also the added benefit of the shilling each that Mum usually gave to Joe and me before ladling most of the rest into her purse. Two coins were placed on top of the meter in the bottom of the cupboard, and a third was inserted into the slot. This was Mum being ultra-cautious lest anyone was alone in the house when the gas went out.

Only one other person ever opened that meter, and that was when I was 15. Unfortunately the police failed to catch him. Thieves had supposedly helped themselves to the contents of several cash meters on South Road over a six-month period, working through the festive and winter nights when most gas was used. Smart thinking really. We weren't at home when we were robbed, so we'll never know if our burglar had on a stripy top, a Lone Ranger mask and a bag with "Swag" printed on it like all criminals had in the Beano. But he sure knew how to burgle. You almost had to be impressed by how he'd kicked the front door open then looked in absolutely every cupboard, wardrobe, drawer, box, tin, jar, bag, wallet and purse in our house. He was very thorough. Somehow I always thought it was a 'he' and never a 'she'. It was just that I couldn't picture a girl peeing in my Mum and Dad's bed like our burglar did. No, I thought that only a male would do something as horrible as that.

So Charleston's "Raffles" got away with the contents of the gas meter, Mum's eternity ring, Dad's watch he got for twenty years' service on the buses, a string of false pearls, a bottle of whisky, and six tins of McEwan's Pale Ale. Quite a haul! I'd have thought that would have needed two of them. I tried the trick of praying to St. Anthony but nothing ever came back.

Although they were upset at losing some of their possessions, it was the peeing in the bed that got to Mum and Dad. That offence to their privacy couldn't easily be repaired, even after they'd changed the sheets, then changed the mattress, then ultimately changed the bed. If they could have, I'm sure they would have changed the bedroom. Even I felt a bit funny at seeing my drawers open when I hadn't opened them myself and my schoolbag tipped up with the contents on the linoleum.

The police told us they believed that our burglar was an opportunist looking to supplement his New Year drink funds and not the professional thieves who were robbing the other houses. It seemed that the other burglars had got into peoples' flats by climbing up into the attics via the hatch at the top of the stairs, then kicking a hole through the ceilings of the top-floor flats. After that, Dad put a great big heavy padlock on the hatch to the attic.

Once again I found myself admiring their cunning as I certainly couldn't have worked out how to get into a locked flat myself. I began to realise some burglars were pretty smart people, with clever ways to get into people's houses and ideas where to look once inside. The bit I couldn't understand was why some of them preferred to pee in people's beds when they could have used the toilet.

Certainly, after being burgled, we felt slightly less safe in our tenement flat, but there was so little crime in our area that we looked at the theft as something unlikely ever to happen again. And it didn't. Nevertheless, Dad added a mortise lock to the front door, requiring a big, long key to turn the deadbolt. The burglary also killed off the tradition of hanging a Yale key on a piece of string behind the letter-box, from where it could be retrieved to open the door.

This system was used at 44 Princes Croft in Coupar Angus where Auntie Mary and Uncle Stan lived with my three cousins Catherine (Renée), Wee Mary and Peter. I remember Renée being very angry with her sister years before, when she found out that Wee Mary had deliberately wound the key string round the inside door handle before going to bed, leaving her big sister with no option but to rouse her parents well after midnight on returning from some romantic tryst. Renée naturally got a good telling-off for being home so late while, eyes closed, her sister enjoyed every moment from the comfort of the bed they shared.

I knew several people whose doors were never locked during the daytime, but there wasn't much worth stealing from most homes. Many folk were entirely dependent on their pensions or family allowance.

Cousins Mary & Renée Grayson

Everyone found the family allowance benefit useful to make ends meet, especially those families with more than a couple of children. Mrs. Bell below us at No. 593 had five or six. Two closes up, Pots Jenkins's Mum had four. At No. 587, Mrs. Brown had four or five and Mrs. Mulholland had five or six, I can't remember exactly. But that paled into absolute insignificance compared to two Catholic families we knew in Wellburn Street behind the Convent. The McLaren clan, of whom Peter was in my first year class at Lawside and Danny was a classmate of my brother, numbered about a dozen, while next door was the Mills family with fourteen children!

With perhaps a single exception, I can't think of any Dads in our area that didn't have a job. Although the Jute industry was in serious decline by the mid-60s, Dundee had attracted some quality replacements, notably NCR (later producer of the world's first cash dispensers), Timex, Veedor Root, Levi Strauss and Valentines greeting cards. There were jobs aplenty for anyone who wanted one and that meant everyone, as it was considered a bit of an embarrassment not to have paid employment. Most Mums however seemed to stay at home looking after the kids and preparing for the return of their husbands from work. We got by on Dad's wage as a busman and the family allowance, although Mum did have the odd part-time cleaning job, for example down at the Linoleum factory.

As a woman, domestic chores in a block of flats like ours meant Mum not only keeping her own house in order but ensuring that the fabric of the tenement was kept up to an acceptable standard, including the stairs, the common close, the drying green and the garden plot. At No. 593 we had five other families in our block and everyone took their turn washing the stairs and walls (walls without graffiti) as well as using the drying green only on their allocated day. Exceptionally the Mums would swap days to use the green round the "backies", if for instance there was illness in the family and bed linen had to be changed more frequently.

In these fairly sheltered circumstances we all felt pretty happy and safe living in our housing scheme in west Dundee. That meant there was no pressing need for us to treat others with suspicion, and there was a degree of innocence that we only shed as our teenage years progressed. Isolated incidents, like our burglary, would speed that process up a bit, but in general our lives were trouble-free and we usually slept soundly in our beds.

30

Change

Where does naughtiness come from? Why do you start being naughty? And how does naughtiness escalate into badness as the years go on? These are hard questions.

Wee Georgie had been a Good Boy pretty much all his life. OK, I know some folk would say that killing a poor rabbit and all those innocent birds was a bad thing to do and I realised later on that I shouldn't have done it. And I also know I could just blame big brother Joe for leading me astray, but that wouldn't be fair either. But certainly compared to many kids I knew, I was reasonably honest, charitable and well-behaved. I suppose the Catholic upbringing I'd had meant there wasn't much likelihood of me being otherwise. "Do unto others as you would have done unto yourself" covered almost all of it in terms of how my mother expected me to conduct myself.

So tracing my transformation into an average teenager is a bit more difficult than it sounds, but it did happen and I can think of some things that contributed to it. I'd spent over five years seriously considering becoming a priest, until Aberfan happened and I dropped the idea. So I guess I was released from any obligation to behave as I imagined a potential priest should. That meant my adolescence was now more like anyone else's.

Naturally I started to copy people around me, especially those older than me. That was definitely the case with smoking. Mum and Dad smoked in the house and I found the sight of them with a cigarette in their mouths quite natural and inoffensive. Joe must have started smoking when I was about eleven and he'd smoke outside the house at every opportunity. It was a bit hypocritical that our parents wouldn't have approved at all if they'd known he'd started to do it too. Knowing that, I kept secret the fact that I'd experimented by smoking cinnamon sticks at the Charleston shops and then later had tried a real cigarette behind Auntie Mary's house.

This, as smokers will recognise, was enough to get me smoking on a daily basis by second year at school, and that was me hooked for the next twelve years. Surprisingly, although he started before me and therefore qualifies as a major influence, Joe never encouraged me to copy him and I'd hazard a guess that, like Mum and Dad, he felt obliged to disapprove. Anyway, he definitely never offered me one of his own cigarettes.

To avoid detection at school where smoking was a multiple-belting offence, my mates and I all developed the skill of holding the filter end between thumb, forefinger and middle finger and folding it back into the palm of the hand, almost but not quite touching the skin. This cradle allowed us to put our hands back in our pockets and look innocent when the duty-teacher came bursting into the toilets of St. Peter's block where we often went for our break-time puff. This technique was wonderfully effective in saving us from frequent beltings.

If smoking was an example of loss of innocence, so also was swearing. The difference here is that this second transgression had absolutely nothing to do with my family, as nobody in it used bad language regularly. Within the Burton and Casciani tribes, relatives expressed outrage with expressions such as *"bloody"* or *"swine"* or, in exceptional cases, *"bloody swine!"* but that's as far as the swearing went. Dad used the typical Yorkshire swear word *"bugger"* pronounced kind of like *"boogah"* but that was considered very mild indeed up here in Scotland. Even with a drink on them, my relations seldom resorted to bad language, and those folk who used it habitually outside our family were regarded as being people of inferior upbringing.

It would be reasonable to say that using foul language came to me from my pals, both in Charleston and at Lawside. We all felt we sounded more mature if we threw the odd curse into the conversation, but of course that would be outdoors on the playing fields or in the street. It was absolute taboo to use such an utterance at home or in a friend's house because most of my pals' parents were quite like ours. Amongst us lads, using the F word gradually became common both as a verb and as an adjective, but the C word somehow never managed to push its way into our vocabulary. When people used it we were still shocked. What we did use a lot was the collection of other slang terms for the sexual parts of the body and things you might get up to with these parts, but that was considered to be perfectly normal by teenage boys going through puberty.

Puberty, inconveniently starting at a different time for each of us boys, led me into naughtiness that simply had to be hidden from parents, even if in the early stages it was all about my thoughts. Then at church I saw a booklet by The Catholic Truth Society that said according to the Bible bad thoughts were the equivalent of bad acts. That was a bit of a shocker. I had no control over the constant sexual images flooding my brain from about the age of thirteen, so I was wracked with guilt for being so evil, but in the end I logically concluded that I might as well do what I was already damned for thinking about!

In September 1968, a month before his eighteenth birthday, Joe registered at St Andrews University, bought a red student gown second-hand, and with a generous Local Authority grant of £360 moved into the annexe of Southgait Hall of Residence for his first academic year. From that day, apart from his odd hitchhike over to visit us and sleeping at home during summer jobs, I had a room all to myself. This was not only life-changing for Joe. It gave me privacy for the first time in my life, a space for myself and the right to do what I wanted inside. I just can't overstate that feeling of freedom.

However, being alone in my room meant I couldn't blame Joe if Mum smelled tobacco smoke, so I adopted a cunning plan I'd seen on TV. This involved hollowing out the bulk of the pages of an old book, lining the cavity with the foil from a few cigarette packs and then taking it with me to bed. At the sound of Mum or Dad approaching I'd pop my fag into the book, close it and hide it under the bedspread. It was sometimes even still alight when I retrieved it once I was again alone. This ridiculous and very dangerous ploy worked perfectly for me and I was never challenged once, although how my parents didn't smell the smoke in my room I'll never know. I put it down to them being smokers too.

Like all my pals, I gradually accumulated a secret stash of illicit 'reading' material. It started with glamour poses from *"Reveille"* or *"Parade"*, moved up to books with a bit of sexual content like *"Valley of the Dolls"*, and then got more sweatily serious with copies of *"Playboy"* and its rivals like *"Mayfair"*. My hiding place was behind the hardboard bath surround, keeping my collection firmly out of sight and accessible only by stretching an arm down the gap where the curve of the bath met a corner of the bathroom. My naughty secret worked a treat…… until the day my folks had to call in a plumber who removed the surround to search for a leak. Thank God I'd left home by then.

Meanwhile I was of course being corrupted in the good old Scottish tradition by alcohol. Again, I can't blame my parents as I wasn't allowed to put my lips to any alcohol in their presence until I was about 17, with the exception of sucking the froth off my Mum's occasional Sweetheart Stout. Cousins Renee, Mary or Peter might smuggle me a tin of Tartan Special out of the bedroom window at the New Year in Coupar Angus, but even then it was one tin and no more.

Things were different outside of home though. Even at 15 years old I found myself drinking beer in a bar, thanks to Jay, my friend of that time who had the look of an eighteen-year old. From a very young age he'd started going to a bar one floor up in the Royal Hotel on Union Street and he eventually invited Dougie Mullen and me to go with him after school, probably once he reckoned we were mature enough to pass for older than we were. With school blazers and ties safely inside our bags, we sat at a table in a quiet corner and Jay brought over half-pints of lager and lime. He pulled out a pack of San Moritz menthol; we all lit up and sat back looking as relaxed as we could, one eye on the door lest Mr Chaplain should walk in for a post-school pint.

As time went on we got bolder and started frequenting the Ascot pub in the town centre and two or three Lochee bars including Mrs. Kidd's, and the Corner Bar up Kirk Street where we played darts. And on Sundays when the pubs were shut we could even sneak into Graystane's Hotel at the start of the carriageway to Perth.

To finance my new racy lifestyle, I came up with a sure-fire money-making scheme which brought in much needed extra cash for Charlie Maclean and me over a period of several months. The concept was brilliantly simple. At that time there was a hugely popular new cartoon on TV called "Wacky Races" in which various strange characters raced each other to a pre-determined finish line while the anti-hero Dick Dastardly and his dog Muttley laid traps to sabotage the efforts of the others and ensure victory for themselves.

Except that Dick and his dog always came unstuck and failed at the last moment while one of the others (my favourite was the Ant Hill Mob!) would win the race to the chequered flag. Each week, "One of the others" was an unknown factor and it was this very point that we exploited.

Having quite a bit of experience with betting odds from my interest in horse-racing, I persuaded

Charlie that we could offer odds on the competitors in the race each week, including an outrageous 100-1 on Dick Dastardly and Muttley in "The Mean Machine". I calculated the odds on the basis of previous race results and my suspicion that the producers of the cartoon would never let the anti-hero win. He never did, always ending with his trademark lament "Drat!! Drat!! And Double Drat!!"

We found it particularly easy to persuade our school friends to part with their spare dosh and have a flutter on the outcome of this American cartoon. Most weeks we'd make a pound or so on Dick Dastardly bets alone and overall we made a tidy profit of a couple of quid per race, although we only broke even the week the incredibly popular Penelope Pitstop in the "Compact Pussycat" stormed to victory.

Our money-tree was chopped down by Jimmy Chaplain when word of our little scheme accidently reached the staffroom one week. The business was compulsorily mothballed, but Chappy was good enough to make an admiring comment on our acumen before closing us down. "Drat!! Foiled again!!"

In the course of the three years between 1967 and 1970, I changed from a pious wee boy with aspirations of embracing the priesthood to an ordinary teenager with all the usual vices, taking pains to keep the truth from my parents. On Hogmanay 1968 I left home a boy and came back a man. The details are best left untold but at last I knew what all the fuss was about.

In addition to my new status, I smoked, drank alcohol, read dirty books, lusted after girls, used swear words and even started missing my night prayers if I could ignore my conscience. I did all that because it's what my friends were doing and though I still worked pretty hard at my schoolwork, I'd had more than enough of being seen as swotty wee Georgie Burton.

It worked.

31

Eccentric

Dougie, Philip and I had a mutual friend who had been quietly in the background all the way through Primary School at St. Mary's Lochee but who metamorphosed very quickly into a strikingly eccentric character within our first two years at Lawside.

Jay was clearly different from the rest of us. Very different. Where we read comics and played guitar, he attended auctions and bought stuffed owls and surgical equipment. By the time he was fourteen, he could be seen walking around Lochee wearing a fedora hat and smoking multi-coloured Russian Sobranie cigarettes. His home was like a menagerie, full of unexpected pieces of furniture and drawers overflowing with the most amazing collection of items, everything from baby lizards in preserving fluid to a monocycle and a crossbow.

For all that, we got on very well with him and the four of us formed a close little group who spent time together both in and out of school, although Jay was often "unavailable" in the evening and at the weekend. He'd tell us he was busy with business at the auctions and it's true he was rarely short of a few bob compared to our too-often empty pockets. He was quite generous to us though, and would share his cigarettes during the week at school and buy us the odd bottle of coke if we went downtown together. The fact that he always seemed to have plenty of money helped compensate in our minds for the strangeness of his character and the way he dressed.

One evening, Dougie and I turned up at his door intending to invite him for a stroll around Lochee Park. Jay greeted us at the threshold and we were surprised to see he had his fedora in his hand. Now this was the first time he'd come out with us wearing it, but he explained that he was going to have to quickly visit a "friend" to pick up some money owed to him for an electric fire he'd sold. So we accompanied him to a wee flat in deepest Lochee where he knocked loudly on the door. There was no response and he shouted through the letter-box that he expected his money immediately.

Dougie and I were naturally ill-at-ease when he did that and we suggested to Jay that he leave things be and return later. Totally ignoring our advice, Jay suddenly unzipped his flies and pushed himself hard up against the door! We looked on in astonishment as he proceeded to pee through the letter-box and into the person's hallway. We were down the stairs and along the road in seconds, aware that what was going on was well over our heads and certainly not something we wanted to be involved with. We decided we'd get an explanation from him the following day at school.

Jay told us his story in a matter-of-fact way that revealed he was living in a world we hardly knew existed. Jay had sold the fire to the man (quite an old man it appeared) at a handsome profit, having acquired it for a few pennies at an auction. The buyer had promised to pay by a certain date and time, but he hadn't done so and wouldn't answer the door when Jay turned up with us to get his money. He wanted to make it clear that this was unacceptable so had chosen to leave a message. Perfectly reasonable. It wasn't the first time he had left such a message and he assured us it wouldn't be the last. Right then I made a mental note never to borrow anything from him.

My eccentric friend wasn't all darkness and mystery. Indeed, mature well beyond his years, he had a wicked sense of humour and great talents, one of which was a particular skill on the piano and keyboard. That's why I worked closely with him when our boys' class were told by Form Teacher Jimmy Chaplain that there would be a special class Mass in a couple of weeks and we were expected to prepare the hymns by writing religious lyrics to modern tunes. Having recently learned The Beatles' *"Yesterday"* on guitar, I decided to change the song title to *"Tranquillity"* and alter Paul McCartney's words to create a plea for peace in the world. Chappy was well-pleased with my efforts.

Jay however had a prowess on the organ that suited another possibility that was spinning about in my head, so I went to his house for a couple of evenings and we worked on the ridiculously-ambitious idea of making a hymn for communion time in the Mass using the song *"Fire"* by The Crazy World of Arthur Brown. Now this tune was already regarded as a bit wild and racy and the sight of the said Mr. Brown jumping around singing it with a burning crown on his head had made us all sit up and take notice, so maybe using it to make a church hymn was a step too far. However, as the alternative lyricist, I excelled myself with some really quite devout words and the title *"Communion"*. So, on the day of the Mass at Lawside, upstairs in the chapel above the staff room, not only did we all sing *"Tranquillity"* and pray for world peace, but Jay bashed out *"Communion"* on the organ while we threw ourselves into the madness of possibly the world's most inappropriate song for a religious service. Jimmy Chaplain took it all in his stride, as usual.

Perhaps it's unfair to lay the entire blame at Jay's door but I had taken to "plunking" with him, sneaking out of school in mid-afternoon to avoid the last couple of lessons and heading off somewhere for a laugh and a smoke. Our destination was often the upper slopes of the

Dundee Law towering over the city to the north. We reasoned that even if Chappy or any other teacher noticed our absence they wouldn't be likely to search for us up on Dundee's extinct volcano. If they did, we were sure to spot them coming long before they could see us. So we would relax in the grass on the north side of the hill, gazing down to the left on St. John's High School and our own Lawside Academy and to the right the two football stadiums of Dens and Tannadice, famously both on the one street.

One pleasant June day with little happening to hold our interest at Lawside, we'd slipped quietly out of the gate on School Road and made our way along the old Newtyle railway track and up the slope of the Law, where we sat down in the sunshine to have a smoke. Charlie Maclean and I got out our packets of No.6 while Jay rummaged in his pockets before producing a new lighter, one of those square bulky ones with a big wick that burned the fuel slowly with a broad high flame. Cigarettes lit and the first drags inhaled, we started to mess around with the lighter, admiring its "lights first time every time" reputation and of course trying to prove it wrong.

Inevitably we began applying the large flame to the grass around us, watching it take fire then stamping it out with our school shoes. Suddenly Jay was up on his feet and lighting the dry grass every two yards or so, shouting how it would be fun to

270

get the Fire Brigade out. Before we could react, the breeze had joined all the little fires up and there was a semicircle of flame between us and our way down the hill. We could see the situation was out of hand and bolted down the Law by the road on the south side. Even before we reached the bottom, we heard the sirens in the distance. By the time we had walked round to Byron Street at Rockwell School, a dozen hefty firemen were beating the hell out of the flames a hundred feet above us. They quickly got things under control, but Charlie and I felt a bit guilty despite the adrenalin rush. Jay on the other hand just enjoyed the thrill with no thought at all to the trouble we'd caused.

Things came to a head unexpectedly one evening at our house in South Road. Dougie, Philip, Jay and I had gathered there because Mum and Dad were going out to the Bingo at the Rialto in Lochee, so we'd have an adult-free evening to smoke, swear and talk openly. Our main goal that night was for Dougie to learn the guitar strumming for *"House of the Rising Sun"* which had been a huge success for The Animals. After bashing out a few tunes we could already manage, we turned our minds to that song. Philip was just sitting in front of the fire on the sofa and Jay was partially out of sight on a chair behind it.

After a few minutes of trial and error, Dougie said he was ready to have a proper go at the tune so he

271

struck up with A minor and picked out the notes. As we finished the first verse (I was singing, Dougie was playing, Philip was watching) we heard some strange sounds from behind us and turned round to see what was going on. Unbelievably, Jay was sitting stark-naked on the chair, head tipped back and moaning quietly. What in God's name was going on? Shocked, I asked him what he was doing. He looked me right in the eye and just told us that he found it impossible to keep his clothes on when he heard that song we'd been playing. He made no move to get his clothes back on and sat speaking to us in the nude. We were all trying to persuade him to get dressed, when suddenly we heard the door opening. Mum and Dad were back early!

This changed the situation dramatically. The three of us leapt back onto the sofa while our naked friend tried unsuccessfully to get into his pants. When the living-room door opened and Mum stepped in, Jay was still trying to cover up what he'd been displaying. Mum took one look, despite her shock screeched "You! Get out! This is a blessed house!" and shrank aside to allow the barely-dressed lad to rush past her and Dad, out the door and down the stairs. Back in the house the five of us just stared at each other, no-one quite able to think of anything to say.

Eventually Dad took control, sent Mum to the bedroom to have a lie down and started to grill us about what we'd been up to and whether anything bad had happened. When he heard our explanation that Jay had said he was powerless to resist the sound of that song, he raised his eyebrows in obvious disbelief, but ultimately he accepted that what we were telling him had the ring of truth. He told Dougie and Philip's parents later on just in case there was more to this than met the eye and Jay was banned from our house and our company.

From then on at school, we were expected to steer clear of this strange boy and there was never a question of being in his company again in the evenings or at the weekend, though we still had to share some lessons with him. Despite what had happened, neither Dougie nor I was particularly upset as we hadn't felt threatened by Jay in any way, but we knew in this case to follow parents' orders and stay away from him. Jay however was unhappy with us not speaking to him anymore and decided to get his revenge. This took the form of some toffees tendered as a peace offering to Charlie and me one lunchtime. We accepted in good faith, ate the sweets and went off to Mr. Minto's Latin class, from which we were both forced to dash without permission some 45 minutes later. The sweets had been injected with strong laxative. Fortunately for us, the boys' toilets were just outside his room at the top of the stairs, so we both made it in time. But only just!

After that, Jay disappeared from my life other than when he routed both Charlie and me in the middle of the Kingsway roundabout where we had lured him to get even. His lifestyle had clearly forced him to learn how to handle himself and he was more than a match for the two of us. The fact we knew he carried a knitting-needle on a cork handle inside the sleeve of his jacket made our attempted attack all the more foolhardy. We really should have let sleeping dogs lie.

32

Jobs

Once I'd turned 16 in February 1969 I was able to look for a job at the weekends and during the school holidays. At that time it wasn't terribly difficult to pick up work somewhere and my search for a Saturday job ended on the first day, when I popped into Willerby the Tailor and was asked to start immediately. I really liked my new working status and the boss thought I had a nice manner with the customers, especially persuading them to add a new shirt and tie to the suit they'd just signed up for.

That job came crashing to an end several weeks later. I was standing at one of the desks (alone unfortunately) when a young man beckoned me over to a rail of trousers he appeared to be browsing. As I came close, I recognized him as one of Dundee's most notorious street-fighters. He carefully opened his long overcoat to reveal his own right arm bent at ninety degrees and in my shock I failed to notice if his right sleeve actually had anything in it.

Cool as you like he ordered me to sling a pair of trousers over his arm, unless I wanted Dundee to be an uncomfortable place for me when the shop closed. I did as he'd asked, he closed his overcoat again and he quietly walked out of the shop with his "purchase" safe inside. For a couple of minutes I was dumbstruck and I just had no idea what I was supposed to do now that he had gone.

Unfortunately, and for not the first time, I chose the absolutely wrong option by reporting the incident to the floor manager, who went ballistic and dashed out of the shop in search of the thief, who had well made his getaway by then. When the manager returned he screamed in my face "You're fired!" and that was that. First job gone. I left with my head held low but 15 minutes later I had a new Saturday job doing the same thing just down the road at the Claude Alexander shop. I managed to hold on to that job for many Saturdays to come, even though their behind-the-scenes facilities left an awful lot to be desired.

I got my first summer job in July of 1969 just after sitting my "O" Grade exams. These had gone to form and hadn't caused me or my friends any great problems, but of course we knew that our "Highers" the following year would be much tougher. My brother Joe had spent the previous summer working in a woollen mill owned by the Scott family on Dock Street. He had put in a good word for me and a couple of my pals, so we all started there the first week of July.

The function of this woollen mill was to take in freshly-shorn fleeces from the farms, grade each fleece into one of 40-50 categories, put batches of similar wool into bales and send them off to wherever. The grading was done by only two old men greatly experienced in how to correctly grade a fleece according to length, thickness, lanolin content etc. These two codgers did their clever work on floor three of the factory.

To get the bags of fleeces up there, we had to use the most dangerous hoist you could ever imagine. It ran the full three floors up and down through what was basically a hole in the floors. We had to manhandle the bags off the lorries, wheel them over to the shaft using long-handled barrows and a hand-held twin hook, fix a rope around each bag and then pull on a rope that activated the pulley motor, hauling the bag upwards to one of the higher floors.

The clever bit (the most dangerous bit too) was to get the heavy bag, which was now swinging like a hanged man's corpse over the shaft, on to the required floor. This was done by a worker on that floor leaning out into the shaft space, digging a hook into the bag and using it to swing the bag to and from the edge. The endangered operative would then tug on the pulley rope to release the tension at the right moment, allowing the bag to drop to the floor beside his feet.

This method of getting heavy bags of wool up two or three floors was fraught with peril, mainly because the actuating rope was a single one whose release was governed only by the strength of the tug on it. It certainly was crazy. On more than one occasion I watched as one of my colleagues found himself being lifted up into the air instead of the bag coming down, because he had pulled too hard on the rope. A gentle pull would release the tension and unwind the pulley, while a harder pull engaged the motor and wound the pulley. The difference? Very little.

We also had to learn to make the bales of graded wool, using an equally scary baling machine that compressed dozens and dozens of fleeces. The empty bale bag was draped inside the head of the machine then turned horizontal to meet up with a long "coffin" filled with fleeces. At the back of this coffin was a ramrod which pushed all the fleeces into the head of the machine. After two pushes, the bag had to be pierced near the top with two sharp steel poles to hold the compressed wool in, tipped back vertical while a jute lid was secured using wooden skewers, then the steel poles were retracted to leave a compressed bale ready for transporting.

This was really hard work, especially inserting and removing the steel poles. If you didn't secure the jute cover well enough then as soon as the poles were extracted the bag would vomit a pillar of wool high into the air in a spectacular explosion. I hated having to force those skewers through the jute in, out and in again as those actions were very hard on my hands and fingers. So despite the inherent danger of working at the hoist, I much preferred to be there than on the baling machine.

The baler had another unofficial function which was to terrify newcomers at their initiation test because you would be placed in the coffin part of the machine, the lid slid into place and the ramrod activated. To avoid being crushed, the newcomer was required to crawl into the empty head of the machine and wait at the bottom at the spot the ram couldn't reach. Now wasn't that fun!

Working with the "daggins" was another adventure which took place in a warehouse on the opposite side to the factory. This was the wool shorn from around the sheep's rear-end so it arrived in heavy bags already contaminated. They were sent up a belt to an attic floor where they dried out and were raked thereafter to rescue the released wool from the sheep droppings. In the summer the methane build-up sometimes led to bouts of spontaneous combustion, as the gas was ignited from the high temperature within. I never actually discovered what happened to all those little bits of reclaimed wool, but I'm sure nothing was wasted.

The mice in the factory were kept at bay by a couple of champion mousers who strolled around the place as if they owned it. These cats were certainly well-cared for and held in quite high esteem by the owners and workers, but they were rarely fed to ensure they did their main job of catching mice. Unfortunately, after various short romances, a litter of kittens would appear and one of the full-time labourers had the job of disposing of all but perhaps one of them. I saw him do this that summer and I was appalled as he casually held one fluffy ball after another down in a great barrel of rainwater. I see that scene to this day.

My friends and I learned a lot during that first working summer, discovering what really was expected of you when you were employed by someone to carry out specific tasks. We learned that, despite our education, our opinions were not required. We learned that not instantly doing as requested by a boss could lead to dismissal. We learned that long hours of hard graft were expected by employers who had no obligation to thank us when we were after all being paid to do the work. And we learned that a punch in the face resolved disputes between workers as often as a conversation round a table.

By my third summer at Scott's woollen mill I was a temporary boss, charged with regulating the invoices from the farmers when they brought in their fleeces, ensuring the amounts tallied and signing off their deliveries. I was paid slightly more for what amounted to less physical labour and that point was not lost on me. If I could impress any future prospective employers by my attentiveness and initiative, I might just be able to avoid the worst excesses of physical effort whilst actually getting more in my hand at the end of the week.

Of all that happened down there on Dock Street, the thing I most disliked was the awful smell that would swamp the factory day after day, a dreadful odour of things unseen and best unspoken emanating from the adjacent slaughterhouse in Market Street. I never went in; I never saw anything, but that smell spoke volumes as to what went on there. It was a similar smell to the one that came from the chicken factory down the road from Auntie Mary's in Coupar Angus. The smell of death.

We were all very excited when we heard there was an escaped cow charging up and down Dock Street one day, causing havoc and bringing traffic to a standstill. We were allowed to go out briefly to take in the scene. It was absolutely brilliant watching this poor beast, clearly clever enough to have realised what was about to befall it, determined to do all in its power to get back to quietly munching grass in a wee field somewhere. In the end however, the authorities gave up trying to catch it and shot it.

At least it gave us something exciting to talk about as we ourselves diced with death at the hoist.

33

Dancing

Around the beginning of 1968, I started going to the dancing along with Charlie Maclean. Now that I'd actually had a proper date, I felt a whole lot more confident about being in the company of girls and I was discovering that making them laugh really did get you somewhere. Better looks would have helped but, failing that, I had to rely on my patter to get a girl interested in the first place. Quite often it was Charlie who made the first move on some unsuspecting female and I was expected to distract her pal enough to let him apply his seduction techniques. He did the same for me but not nearly as often as I did that job for him.

Charlie Maclean

The main venue for our chasing of girls was the J.M. Ballroom on North Tay Street. We had started off by attending "The Tufty Club" (named after the iconic road-safety squirrel) on Tuesdays from 7-10 p.m. which was the venue for younger teenagers to meet up. We quickly tired of that, thinking we were all oh so mature and looking for older girls. So we started going to "The Rave Cave Club" on Monday nights and soon we couldn't wait for that session to come around each week. By fifth year at school we were going there on Saturday nights as well. Of course, there were specific requirements for going to the dancing, and these essentials started changing us even more.

To get into the J.M. you had to be smartly dressed. This meant that I had to get some decent clothes to wear, so I had to work hard on Mum and Dad to cough up the price of a shirt and tie or new shoes to go with the suit I'd be wearing. My wages for delivering papers were lasting me no time at all. At that point my pals were all buying made-to-measure suits from Burton's or Jackson's and I was no exception. I was measured up for a grey double-breasted suit with a Regency collar, all a bit Carnaby Street, but it had the desired effect and improved my chances of pulling a girl.

It went without saying that I also had to be clean and tidy for going out so I was constantly scrubbing my face to keep the spots down to a mere plague. My now shoulder-length hair was being washed every night to counteract the grease in which it appeared to love to coat itself. Wasn't puberty great fun? Luckily for me, Mum came up with an old Indian trick one night when I was short of time and hurrying to get ready. She told me to sprinkle talcum powder on my hair then brush it through. In desperation I gave it a try and would you believe it, it worked! No more greasy hair. From then on I always had some Johnson's Baby Powder in the bathroom just in case.

Actually getting into the J.M. wasn't as easy as you might imagine because they always had a squad of bouncers on the door and these guys had to be taken seriously. One of them had even been a contestant in the Mr. Universe competition. Their main job was to ensure that no-one got in if they appeared to have been drinking, as the ballroom had a strict "no alcohol" policy. As the queue (there was always a queue) reached the entrance, you had to climb three or four steps and go in by the middle door of three, then turn right as directed by the first bouncer to reach the cash desk a couple of yards ahead.

To the right of the cash desk there was another door through which you'd be conducted if the second bouncer on duty suspected that you'd been drinking. That door brought you back out at the top of the steps, exposed to the ridicule of those still in the queue. If you resisted or objected, you were "assisted" out of the door and down the steps by the bouncer. On more than one occasion after two or three pints in the Ascot, I found myself flying down the steps to make a rather undignified landing on the pavement below.

My pal Ricky Gierelo

On one particular evening I had waited with Charlie Maclean and Ricky Gierelo, another close friend and JM-goer, for almost two hours in a long queue in the cold and wind to get into the J.M. for the hugely-anticipated Morgan School Dance, where there was always an exceptional array of unattached girls. Unfortunately I'd been suffering from a by now rare attack of Hay Fever and had applied Optrex in an eye-bath to afford myself some relief before going out. The cold wind in my

285

face did nothing to make the situation any better, meaning that when I reached the entrance door, the bouncer took one look at my eyes and nodded to his colleague two yards away. I gasped in horror as the dreaded second door was pulled open and I was invited to leave. How unfair was that?

But on most occasions, even when we'd had a pint or two, Charlie, Ricky and I would manage to get in with no fuss and, after depositing our coats at the cloakroom, we'd go into the main dance hall to see what was on offer. The standard procedure was for the girls, in pairs and small groups, to dance together in the middle with their bags at their feet. The boys circulated around them, sizing up the prey and preparing to make their move. The usual procedure was a bold stride into the dance area, a tap on the selected girl's shoulder and a big smile. You could usually judge from the girl's face if the first impression was good. You knew for certain it wasn't if she immediately shook her head and turned her back on you.

At the end of the first dance, you could ask the girl if she wanted to "stay up" with you and keep dancing or return to her friends. If she agreed to another dance there was a fair chance you'd pulled, and might end up taking her home or snogging her outside the dance hall. To seal the alliance, it was normal to invite the girl to go upstairs for a chat and a drink (no alcohol of course) and the beginnings of romance often blossomed over that first glass of Coca-Cola.

Rejection was quite a likely result of asking a girl to "stay up" but we'd simply move on to the next girl and try our luck again. It was awkward if Charlie, Ricky or I found a girl whose friend wasn't keen on the other of us. This led to "male friend versus girl" decisions but the truth is that the male friends got dumped almost every time and the successful chatter-up would walk away with the spoils, leaving his less lucky pals to try the Lone Wolf method or pack it in and go home. However, even if earlier approaches had been unsuccessful, there was always the final chance of getting off with a girl at the last dance, which was always slow or smoochy.

This involved anticipating the dimming of the lights, leaving as the only illumination the huge glitter ball dangling from the middle of the ceiling, then making for your target before she had time to bend down to retrieve her bag and head for the cloakroom. This ploy quite often worked as the girl was either too surprised to object or relieved that she hadn't been spurned for a slow dance at the end of the night.

Coming out of the J.M. was sometimes quite scary. Firstly it was just possible that the boyfriend (or husband) of the female you had your arm around could be standing outside waiting for her. That only ever happened to me once, a rejected ex-boyfriend making a last effort to win back the love of his life, despite the fact that I was on her arm and she wasn't letting go. Fortunately he left peaceably but broken-hearted. The second problem was that members of gangs would sometimes line the wall on the other side of Marketgait from the J.M. and study the young folk as they left, hoping to spot someone they had it in for. Luckily I was never a target but I kept my radar on red-alert until I was on the bus home or all the way up the Lochee Road, Ancrum Road and Charleston Drive on foot as was very often the case.

The musical entertainment in the J.M. was provided by a resident live band and one or two guest groups. We were never very impressed with the house band, even though they were highly accomplished and had to learn all the latest hits so quickly. The residents were called the *Pat'r 4* and when they added two girl dancers to gyrate in front of them they of course became the *Pat'r 4 + 2*. They even moved on later to become the *Pat'r 4 + 3*! Over the three years we went there, we got to know which bands were not to be missed, including the *Poets* who did a fantastic cover of "I am the Walrus", the *Chris McClure Section* out of which Christian made a successful singing career, and the fantastic *Bay City Rollers*, not the tartan-clad version that conquered the world in the 70s, but a slick white-suited band who needed crash barriers to keep them safe from their adoring groupies. I wasn't envious, of course.

288

Charlie met the lass who would become his wife at the J.M. on a typical night in 1970 when he and I went out dancing in the hope of finding ourselves new female company. Two very tidy girls dancing together caught our eyes and we moved in. Charlie danced with Elaine, a pretty girl with gorgeous long brown hair, while I danced with her pal Carol who sported a lion's mane of ginger hair. Both girls looked interested so we made our play, danced a bit, went upstairs for a drink, danced a bit more then took the girls home. Both lived in Menzieshill but we had to separate at the end as they didn't live right next to each other. I had a great kiss and cuddle with Carol in the common close of her tenement block and the next day at school Charlie told me he had been equally successful. Sometime later, Carol told me that she fancied another of my pals. We split up, she went out with the new bloke, and eventually she married him. Charlie and Elaine became life partners too.

It was straight from the J.M. that I came one fateful evening, complete with a new girl, along with half a dozen of my school friends, each of them with a girl he'd picked up that evening. Perhaps the promise of a party at my parents' house had softened the girls' resistance to our charms, but a very happy group of us walked up Lochee Road, over Ancrum Road into Menzieshill and across the field to 593 South Road. There was an opportunity for me to give a party because Mum and Dad were visiting Coupar Angus and Joe was at University in St.

Andrews. I confess that it was unplanned and I didn't have permission to bring six of my male pals and seven strange girls into our home.

The thing went really well, although when my new girl admitted she was only thirteen (she certainly didn't look that young in makeup!) I had to throw her out, with the lyrics to "Young Girl" by *Gary Puckett & the Union Gap* ringing in my ears. There was no mess, everybody was gone by ten in the morning and when Mum and Dad came home they didn't notice anything at all. However, the next morning when Dad went to put on the watch he always left on the chest of drawers at the bottom of his bed, it wasn't there. He searched everywhere and even went next door to phone Auntie Mary to ask if he'd left it in Coupar Angus. No, he hadn't.

Eventually I admitted my guilt and received appropriate punishment for my stupidity. Despite investigations, neither I nor any of my pals ever found out who had stolen the watch, but there would be no more secret parties at the Burton household, that was for sure. At Lawside I knew all the girls and had known some of them for ten years, so there were few surprises there. On the other hand, the girls from the J.M. were all unknown factors from other schools or walks of life. Though one or two of them may not have been too trustworthy, their unfamiliarity helped to enhance the thrill of the chase. We never knew if we would successfully chat up a girl and if we did, we were never quite sure what we were letting ourselves in for. That was so exciting!

Heartfelt thanks to the J.M. Ballroom.

34

Julie

My Mum's eldest sister was Julie, who was so old that her daughter Mary was second oldest child of my generation in the extended family of which I was the youngest. She lived in Aboyne Avenue with her husband Wull Blacklock, in the housing scheme we always called Douglas & Angus. Uncle Wull was the man who worked as a uniformed commissionaire at the Regal Cinema in Small's Wynd off Dundee's Hawkhill.

Julie's daughter Mary had a flat around the corner in Kemnay Gardens, where she lived with husband Ronnie Torano and their two children - 'Wee' Ronnie and Ann, both not much younger than Joe and me. It was in their flat that it was decided to hold a bit of a get-together the evening before Julie's funeral, after she had failed to recover from a broken hip sustained in a fall at home. I was competing in the Dundee Easter Chess Congress that year so when I turned up it was to find the family event in full swing.

Once I'd let Mum know how I'd done that day, I set about circulating around my cousins, uncles and aunties catching up with their busy lives and finding out who was going to be married, who was expecting a child and who wasn't keeping so well.

Julie's resilience in living so long was being compared to Grandma's 84-year stint down on planet Earth. It was a family joke that Grandma was so fit and healthy that when she died, the doctor said he couldn't find anything wrong with her.

Dying at an advanced age was therefore quite possible if you were of Casciani stock and that cheered up us younger ones quite a bit. It appeared that if you managed to actually survive being born (which lots of the family babies hadn't) and got beyond the age of three, then there was a fair chance you could count on having your three-score-and-ten or maybe even a bit more. Grandma had reached 80+ and daughter Julie just short of that, while next in line Lizzie was already in her late sixties and fit as a fiddle. The men had fared less well, due in part to the World Wars, although Grandad Casciani had died of bronchitis between them.

Of course, the topic of death and the changes it brings (especially to the deceased) was always inextricably linked to the Catholic religion in our family and it was generally assumed Julie was now in heaven watching us having a party on her behalf. So when the assembled family members started talking about Julie's religious icons which they were going to spread around the family as keepsakes (husband Wull being non-Catholic), I listened closer to what was being said about her rosaries and statues and missals and medals and paintings and souvenirs and Lourdes water. No bible of course. We were Catholic after all.

At some point, Auntie Cissie told the whole room that I was a great fan of the Blessed Virgin Mary and that Julie would definitely have wanted me to have her statue of the Mother of Jesus. This statue was a plaster of Paris one in blue and white, with the Virgin's arms outstretched holding in her right hand the staff of something or other. I felt quite honoured given my lack of years, and accepted the keepsake at once.

What I didn't expect however was that cousin Mary would give me the key to her Mum's house and tell me to go and fetch it there and then. I took the key from her and was just leaving the crowded living room when she added "You won't be scared of your dead Auntie, will you?" I felt my insides twitch violently. I had not appreciated that dear Auntie Julie would still be lying in her coffin in the bedroom of her flat in Aboyne Avenue. And of course, given the family tradition, that coffin would still be open....

After nodding that I wouldn't have a problem, I left Mary's flat and walked out into the common close where I paused to try and pull myself together. How would I be able to go into the late Auntie Julie's house and remove the statue from the head of her open coffin? What if she opened her eyes? What if she grabbed me? What if she sat up and accused me of stealing her statue? Oh no! This was too scary, really. But my problem was that I had to avoid admitting I was too frightened as I would be mercilessly laughed at if I returned without the statue. At age 16 I was seriously trying to be a grown-up and not still wee Georgie, but maybe I'd watched too many horror movies.

Wull and Julie outside 3 Aboyne Avenue

I concluded that there was no choice but to go in, take the statue and run. Assuming dead Auntie Julie did not in fact grab me with her bony hand and pull me into her coffin, I reckoned I could be in and out again in less than a minute. So off I strolled, passing Auntie Mary's window looking as casual as I could and turning left round into Aboyne

Avenue. Julie and Wull's flat was the bottom left of a block of two-up two-downs on the right side of the street. I entered the close, tiptoed up to the door and paused to listen. When I was sure Auntie Julie wasn't walking around inside, I knocked on the door. Why did I do that? Maybe I was waiting for her to shout "Come in!" But for some reason I knocked again. I slowly inserted the key in the Yale lock and turned it, before very carefully pushing the door open and stepping inside.

I planned to leave that door wide open, but to my horror it swung back towards the closed position aided by a kind of spring hinge that lots of old folk had installed on their doors. I grabbed it as it creaked past me and pushed it fully open again. Looking straight ahead I could see the closed living-room door to my right and the open bedroom door to my left. Inside the bedroom, laid on two wooden trestles, was Auntie Julie's coffin. I could just make out her nose sticking up from her blanched face. And behind her head, at the far end of the coffin, there was a tall, thin occasional table, on top of which stood the Virgin Mary statue with staff in hand.

A quick glance around the lobby revealed nothing with which I could jam the front door open. To look for something in another room would obviously mean letting the door shut as I moved away. Taking a deep breath, I prepared to sprint into the room, grab the statue and hopefully get back to the door before it shut. One, two, three, go! I was in the bedroom and up to the head of the coffin in a flash, trying really hard not to look at my Auntie Julie's corpse in case she looked back at me. I stretched over her body and grabbed the statue.

That's when the Virgin Mary's hand moved! I screamed and dropped the statue before fleeing to the now closed front door. I opened it at the second frantic attempt and jumped out into the close. The door closed in front of me. What in the name of all the Saints was that? How could the hand with the staff in it have moved? It was impossible, but it had definitely happened, I was sure. OK. Time to calm down and take stock of the situation. I had to go back with the statue but I'd dropped it in the bedroom where the coffin was. How was I going to get it back?

I gave myself a real shake, turned the key in the lock for a second time, went into the flat and stopped at the entrance to the bedroom, my eyes scanning the floor for the statue, or at least bits of it. Where was it? Where could it have rolled? With all possibilities considered, I quickly came to a conclusion I really didn't want to arrive at. I stretched up on tiptoe and peeked back into the open coffin. Sure enough, there it was, still in one piece, lying against dead Auntie Julie's right cheek! The whole situation was becoming worse and worse, but I was at last feeling less panicked and I forced myself to just go back in and gently remove the statue from the coffin.

As I lifted it, the statue's hand moved again. This time I saw it was only because a pin holding it into the arm was rotating in its hole where it must have cracked at the wrist some time before. More than a little relieved, I gave dearly departed Auntie Julie a final smile, wished her "God bless" and turned to leave. Then as I reached the front door, I thought I heard a noise coming from the bedroom. I admit that I left without investigating further.

Back at Kemnay Gardens, I explained that my tardiness was on account of difficulty getting the lock on the front door to turn. My story was accepted without comment. The truth was known only to Auntie Julie herself, and she wasn't saying anything.

35

Highers

On the 20th of July 1969, Neil Armstrong and Buzz Aldrin left the "Eagle" Lunar Module and walked on the surface of the moon. Some said it was the most important moment in the history of mankind and in truth it was at the very least highly significant.

Fifth Year at Lawside turned out to be very significant too. For the first time in my school career, I had to work really hard to keep pace with the lessons and complete the work on time to an acceptable standard. It was the same for lots of my school pals as well. Until then we had pretty much strolled through our schoolwork, both in the classroom and at home, and most of us had passed 7 "Ordinary" grades without breaking sweat.

But doing "Highers" was very different, as would be summarised in classic fashion by my French teacher, the wonderful John Murphy. Mr. Murphy was admired by teachers and pupils alike for his homespun Dundonian philosophy. His conversation was punctuated with brilliant vernacular phrases for miscreants such as *"Any more o' that and you'll be eatin' yer tea aff the mantelpiece"* or, for late arrivals to his class *"Hey, what do you think this is, the night shift?"* The concept of eating my meal off the mantelpiece kind of left me perplexed until someone pointed out that the diner's bum would be too sore to sit down.

So, on the first day of the Higher French class, as 30-odd of us sat waiting for Mr. Murphy to arrive, all of us equally chuffed at having sailed through "O" grade French *sans problème*, I suppose we were looking for a brief "Well done, boys" at the very least. Lawside wasn't a place you could count on being congratulated all that often, no matter how well you'd done (unless you were in the football team), but we did at least expect a bit of recognition.

With familiar black cloak fluttering behind him, John Murphy burst into the room, strode over to his desk, put down a bundle of books and jotters, turned to his audience of smug faces and said *"O grades? Huh! They give them away wi' Daz coupons!"* He followed this with *"Right, you lot. Get oot a jotter and a pencil. You're gonna do some real work now."* Our self-esteem crashed back to an appropriate level and we searched in our schoolbags for the jotters and pencils. Within minutes we were struggling through a difficult Unseen prose passage, while Mr. Murphy sat at his desk, preparing another even longer one for us to do as homework.

My other four Higher subjects were English, Maths, Latin and German. The latter two were to pass without incident, except for the Latin master Mr.

Burns being the subject of a cruel prank when our class decided to translate Virgil's "Aeneid" using any English word that resembled the Latin one, even if we knew the correct answer. *"Equus"* became "equal" and not "horse" and we all thought this was hilarious. After a few minutes of ludicrously wrong translations, Mr. Burns held his bald pate in his hands in despair and turned his back on us. This reaction brought us back to our senses and we eventually relented. We liked a laugh but we weren't in the business of causing him distress.

Higher English was a delight in the hands of the exceptional Tom Ferrie who opened our eyes to the wonder of William Shakespeare and in particular *"Macbeth"*. He led us through the Scottish Play masterfully, setting us excerpts and soliloquies to learn by heart and letting us act out important scenes on the floor of the classroom. I loved doing that, and I'd already played the part of Oberon, King of the Fairies, in the previous school year's production of *"A Midsummer's Night's Dream"*. Not bad for a wee boy from Parker Street.

When Burns' Night came around in January 1970, my group of friends got together and decided to don full tartan dress for the evening at school. However, we added an unexpected finale to the celebrations by suddenly leaving our seats and exiting the hall in procession, with right arms held aloft, mimicking a sketch from the ground-breaking comedy programme *"Monty Python's Flying Circus"*. In the forthcoming months we'd re-enact many of our favourite sketches in the playground, including the Ministry of Silly Walks. This gave rise to the strange sight of phalanxes of senior pupils goose-stepping in formation round the yard.

Higher Maths was not such a delight once we'd been introduced to the mystery of Calculus, possibly the first thing I ever needed to understand but couldn't. This challenge forced me to call on mental reserves I didn't know I had. Although I scored an "A" in the final exam, I was at my limit with this subject and was really thankful to lay it to rest. I'd been a bit of a swot throughout my schooldays, both primary and secondary, always trying really hard in class and always doing my homework to the best of my ability, especially in Maths which was my strongest subject. But in the Higher class we got a new teacher who was not averse to using the belt to make a point.

I got on his wrong side when, for the first time ever, I forgot to do my Maths homework. Even I couldn't believe it when I opened my jotter to show him I'd done them, only to discover I hadn't. My face must have showed my shock at the oversight. But the Maths teacher showed no compassion, marching me out onto the floor in front of all my classmates and giving me two hard whacks on the hands. Me, a seventeen-year old top pupil with a perfect record in the Maths class up to then, belted by a man who barely knew me. For a single error in 5 years.

I hear many, many people say they were often belted at school and it did them no harm and indeed did them a lot of good. It taught them respect, justice and other laudable intangibles. Blah blah. Yet that single punishment by my Maths teacher had the opposite effect on me. Physically it did me no harm of course, but its unfairness left a scar that was hard to heal. I never forgave him for that.

Prelim exams acted as the intended wake-up call for most of us, a reminder that our focus was meant to be our studies and not the teenage pleasures we were revelling in. It also marked the first time I ever failed an exam (47% in German) and that was just the kick in the pants I required. After the Christmas holidays I needed no further encouragement to apply myself to my Higher subjects, and I plunged even deeper into the "swot" category, refusing invitations to all sorts of nights out and parties. But I could feel the pressure mounting.

To alleviate the stress of intense studying all day, a group of us started taking the school bus into town at 4 o'clock but not immediately jumping on the 28 or 29 to travel back to Charleston. Instead we'd wander down Reform Street and go into the Lite-Bite, a downstairs café in a baker's shop, where we could spend an hour or so over a cuppa and the cake of our choice. I usually had a slice of Millionaire's Shortbread but my favourite was really the Ayton sandwich, that excellent diamond-shaped biscuit with a chocolate cream filling and chocolate-coated base. Sadly, even then they weren't readily available, because by then production had ceased. It was a real tragedy.

Quite often I'd share this down time with my classmate Alice Tully, who slowly became my closest confidante and the sister I'd never had. We regularly ended up eating at each other's house and we'd go from there to studying together, since we shared the majority of our subjects that year. Despite the obvious opportunity for romance to blossom, it never happened between us and we 'mply matured into best friends. Mum was really a. `ppointed at this turn of events and would have haα ` otherwise, but as Alice was already being court᷑ ᷉ by my mate Colin, the situation didn't lend itself to me making a move. I kept my romantic intentions for other girls at Lawside, like Mary Mooney and Ann Dellaquaglia.

At the hundredth time of asking, June Barclay's defence finally crumbled and she agreed to go out to the cinema with me. I was ecstatic and made a particular effort to dress as smartly as possible, shampoo and brush my long hair, hide any spots I still had underneath some of mum's face powder and use mouthwash after brushing my teeth for half an hour. I needn't have bothered. The date went well but when I moved in for a snog, she backed off and let me know that her heart belonged to another boy from school. My own heart cracked right down the middle, but June was genuinely kind to me and let me down as gently as she possibly could. It was OK I suppose.

The rest of the spring and early summer of 1970 was pretty much study, study, study, and soon the Higher exams were over and we could relax again. At the suggestion of a friend, Mick Garty, a group of us started going up to Blairgowrie on a Saturday afternoon, pitching a tent on the near bank of the River Ericht up by Cargill's Leap, then spending the evening in town. This was usually around the Wellmeadow, in the Cartwheel and the Vic ubs, getting merry and chatting up the local girls.

Wellmeadow, Blairgowrie

We'd start the evening with a few games of darts to accompany our pints of Harp Lager, and move on later to the Dreadnought where the jukebox created a musical ambiance more suitable for our intentions. We fell in love with a different girl every week, got chased away by jealous brothers and boyfriends every other week, and sometimes we even made it back to the tent to sleep, if we could navigate the pitch black banks of the Ericht with too much lager in us. In the morning (shame upon us), we would steal bottles of milk from the houses on the opposite bank by crossing the shallow straits above the Leap, shoes and socks in our hands, and then it was time to catch the bus back to Dundee and a quick snooze for me before six o'clock mass at St. Clements's church. Hypocrite? Not me.

The Burtons and family on the banks of the Ericht

When the Higher results came out that August, I had passed all five, with "A" in French and Maths,

"B" in English and German and "C" in Latin. This gave me the group of grades I needed to back up my application to the four Universities I'd selected. York, Warwick and Edinburgh all wanted me, which was brilliant, but when the University of St. Andrews followed suit and accepted me to study French Language & Literature, there was really no contest. I proudly accepted their offer of an unconditional place on the course, to start in September 1971.

With a place at University tied up, I knew my sixth and last year at school was going to be a whole lot of fun, and include as little studying as possible. And so it turned out.

36

CSYS

As I entered my final year at Lawside for my Certificate in Sixth Year Studies, the world was buzzing with the Vietnam War, Apollo 13, and Brazil's triumph in the Mexico World Cup. For me, however, the most important thing was that John, Paul, George and Ringo would never play together again, depriving the planet of the best songs that had ever been. Their last album "*Let it Be*" had lived up to all of its predecessors, especially with the evocative "*Long and Winding Road*" which sounded to me like a final bye-bye from the Fab Four.

That World Cup in Mexico had been special too. The Brazilians moved towards the title displaying a brand of football that we'd quite frankly never seen before. I watched them on TV take the game to a level of artistry that was quite beautiful, so fluid and choreographed were their moves. Pele, the world's greatest player, blew us away with his attempt from the halfway line and his "dummy" against Uruguay, one of the most wonderful things I ever saw on a football pitch. Even today there are many among us who claim that the Brazil team which won the World Cup in 1970 was the best football team of all time.

But back at Lawside I found myself at the centre of a minor controversy. Soon after first term started, Mr. Adams and his assistants put together a list of those pupils they felt should become Prefects. Given my record at school, my name was automatically added to the list for St. Paul's House, but when I went to collect my badge, Mr. Chaplain made it clear that it wasn't available until I'd had a haircut.

Mum didn't mind my long hair!

Now at that time my hair was long and straight, parted to one side and down to my shoulders, like the style of so many current rock stars. As much to my own surprise as to his, I told him that getting a haircut simply wasn't an option. Heavens above, I'd come a long way from the ever-so cooperative and compliant wee Georgie, hadn't I? I wanted things to happen my way now, using my rules, my ideas and my principles, not the school's. So, yes, I'll be a

Prefect, but the hair stays. Chappy listened patiently to my argument then sent me away ...... without a badge and without the title. No haircut, no Prefect.

If the authorities at Lawside felt a little uncomfortable about one of their very top pupils not having the title of Prefect, they certainly didn't show it and for the following two or three weeks the subject was never broached. This left me with no permission to use the Prefects' Room during free periods, intervals and lunchtimes, while all my friends were inside enjoying their new status and continuous cups of coffee. Something had to give here. Of course it was my hair that eventually conceded defeat, although I kept it well over my ears to retain a semblance of dignity in the face of a crushing defeat from the Establishment.

A sixth year of study at school was meant to prepare you for future study at University level, mixing formal classes in advanced topics with greater freedom of choice and private study time, plus regular visits to outside institutions including universities and colleges. Visiting lectures and seminars with pupils from other schools made up my study routine, supplemented by tapes in the Language Laboratory, given that I was supposedly studying French and German along with English.

What actually happened was of course that, with my unconditional offer from the University of St.

Andrews tucked away under my belt, I did as little as I possibly could, arriving late, leaving early, missing classes, taking days off and generally skiving. The death of Jimi Hendrix seemed much more important to my life than a dissertation on the works of Thomas Hardy, how could it not be? Perusing the pages of *"Melody Maker"* and *"New Musical Express"* took up far too much of my time to let me finish any homework tasks by their deadlines. And then the death-knoll of study for CSYS was sounded when some of us got together and formed a band.

This was the next natural step after jamming together for hours in each other's homes, learning the chord sequences for hundreds of songs and practising vocal harmonies. My pal Dougie Reid and I led the way with guitars and vocals, while we were joined by John Duncan on keyboards. This instrument actually belonged to Dougie, who'd bought it from his mum's "clubby book" and was paying it over 18 weeks at 19/11d per week. It seemed to me that everything in Freemans' Catalogue was paid up at 19/11d per week!

As all decent groups had a drummer, we enlisted the help of Ian Rae, who just happened to have a set of drums and a wee van. I'd like to think we added him for his inimitable talent on the drums but that might not be entirely true. Anyway, we rehearsed briefly before getting our first break, playing in the bar at the Inchture Hotel on a Friday night, thanks to P.E. teacher Gerry Devlin who owned that establishment in the nearby village. We did quite well that evening and got a nice round of applause from the six people present. We did one more gig, a Saturday night spot at Blairgowrie Town Hall where holidaying Glaswegians spent the evening kicking the living daylights out of each other. So much for our great set of songs!

The last time we got together was at school for an end of year celebration where the teachers asked us to perform a few songs. We enhanced our line-up by adding the voice of Leng Medal winner Patsy Cosgrove and we chose an eclectic mix of rock and folk, but the audience just sat and listened to the rock and then, thanks to an untimely intervention by Jimmy Chaplain, started to dance to our folk songs. That was very strange for us up on the stage watching school kids shake to "The Wild Mountain Thyme". And after that, just like the Beatles, we split up.

While the Christmas holidays were a bacchanalia for me and my friends with hardly a sober night to speak of, the momentous occasion of my eighteenth birthday on 17 February 1971 turned out to be unusually quiet for me but a bit of an adventure for Mum and Dad.

Two days before that, we had the unique event of the UK saying cheerio to Old Pounds, Shillings and Pence and converting to decimal currency with a hundred new pence to the pound. At a stroke Dougie had to start paying ninety-nine and a half new pence for the keyboard lying unused in the corner of his bedroom. Luckily for him, he managed to offload it to Colin Coupar, the boyfriend of my pal Alice.

This deal had been struck while bringing in the New Year on the roof of the changing rooms in Dawson Park, just along from Colin's house. The negotiation was very brief because we all had to jump off the roof and run away over the frost-covered grass, following the unexpected arrival of the police. We meant no harm but got a stern ticking-off and all our names were noted.

One of my birthday presents in February was of course one of each of the new coins, although we'd been using the five and ten new pence coins for a couple of years already alongside the old money, but the wee coins of two, one and a half new pence were a novelty for us all, as was the very unusual seven-sided 50 new pence.

The plan for my birthday celebration was relatively simple: sometime after tea, Mum, Dad and I would go down to the Gaiety Lounge where I'd be bought my first legal drink. I secretly worried that the excitement would vanish as soon as it became legal for me to drink in a pub, but being bought a drink by my parents was definitely going to be a "first". This made up for the fact that I would receive hardly any birthday cards that year, as a National Postal Strike was well into its fifth week.

Auntie Cissie, Mum and me passing the Gaiety

So, that evening, we had that momentous drink together in the Gaiety, but were joined soon after by Dad's conductor Bert and his wife. At closing time they invited us back to their flat in nearby Gourdie Street, where they intended to sample some bonded rum that Bert had acquired, while I was sent to a bedroom to play guitar with Bert's son who was in bed with the 'flu. This in itself was a strange turn of events but what transpired was even stranger.

When I went back through around midnight to suggest we all go home, it was clear that my parents were unusually merry. Indeed Mum had developed a real fit of the giggles and Dad was having difficulty putting on his overcoat. Well, walking them home was frankly a nightmare, as I had to link the arms of both of them with mine, as we walked past the play park and up Craigowan Road. Getting them up four flights of stairs to our tenement flat in South Road was a real achievement.

I left them to put themselves to bed, still a bit shocked to see my own Mum and Dad in such a state. Mum normally drank very little alcohol and Dad usually stuck to a couple of pints of lager at the weekend, so to see them struggling to walk was a real eye-opener for me. What had there been in that rum?

Anyway I wasn't long in bed myself when I heard a thump followed by Mum laughing out loud. I got up, knocked and went into their bedroom. Mum was lying in bed chuckling away to herself, which I failed to understand until I caught sight of Dad lying on the floor beside his chest of drawers. Silly man. However, when I moved to help him up I was shocked to see a gash in his temple and blood running down his face. He had clearly tried to get out of bed to go to the toilet but his legs had failed him and he'd fallen down, striking his head off the corner of the chest of drawers.

So, my eighteenth birthday finished with me ministering to my inebriated father and the cut on his head, while Mum happily laughed herself to sleep. The following day wasn't easy for either of them but Dad did eventually find out from Bert that the rum they'd been drinking that evening was double the normal proof. That accounted perfectly for why my parents had become so very, very drunk so quickly.

Luckily I never saw Mum or Dad under the influence again after that day.

37

Finale

My last significant moments as a pupil at Lawside came far from School Road in Dundee; more than a hundred miles away in fact, in the Cairngorms.

Teacher Jimmy Chaplain had already established himself as the King of the outward-bound school trip; he had organized a post-examination week for senior pupils in the hostel and Norwegian huts up at Loch Morlich every year since his arrival at Lawside. So when it came time for names to be put forward, as it was our last chance to try out life in the mountains, I signed up along with Dougie, Charlie, Jake, Dodge and the rest of our group. As Chappy had been our Register Teacher for the previous five years, he knew us all inside out and there was little chance that we wouldn't make it onto the final list. And so it transpired.

In late May, with the exams safely behind us (exams I failed miserably for lack of effort), we were driven up north to Aviemore in two minibuses, then east to Loch Morlich and the former Commando huts where we would stay. The bulk of Cairngorm rose to the south, with Ben Macdhui, Cairn Toul and Braeriach beyond and the massive valley of the Lairig Ghru between them. This was very different indeed from our urban environment in Dundee, but naturally we, a group of immortal eighteen-year old boys, assumed we'd master it in a trice. Oh, the folly of youth!

On the second day we were divided into groups for our first hike, a fifteen mile stroll through Glenmore forest around the area of Rothiemurchus. Just before we left, Jimmy Chaplain came over to our group, commented that "Burton" would be smart enough for the role of group leader, and handed me a map and compass. I nodded confidently, called the lads together, explained the route we'd be taking and off we went. Fifteen minutes later we were hopelessly lost in the forest.

To our great misfortune, not only was I useless with the map and compass, but so was every other person in our group. Naturally we all sought to blame each other. I think it was Dodge who suggested that we could find South by looking for the sun, but we were in deepest Glenmore Forest and it was raining, so that didn't help much. Needless to say, we spent the next three hours wandering around looking for paths that weren't there, or finding a path that just took us somewhere equally baffling.

The worst part was trying to cross a huge area of uprooted tree trunks that looked like a gigantic ploughed field with drills three or four feet high. It took us ages to work our way laboriously through that tree cemetery and several of us considered giving in and just sitting down to await rescue. I did however use my persuasive powers as group leader to get everybody to the other side, where I suggested they rest for a while.

I decided to move ahead with Dougie as a partner, looking for a possible way out of this Highland hell. Amazingly, just a hundred yards further on through the trees, we found ourselves on the edge of a huge clearing filled with canvas tents and jeeps and military equipment. We had discovered Rothiemurchus Military Camp. While Dougie walked back to get the others, I went down into the Camp and explained my plight to some soldier or other who quickly organized a transport vehicle to take us back to Loch Morlich.

We were ecstatic on our return and boasted to our friends in the other groups (all of whom had completed their walk without incident) how we had been driven home and hadn't had to walk at all. Jimmy Chaplain obviously noticed our cockiness over tea and resolved to teach us a lesson. So, when everyone on the trip prepared to leave the following day for some leisure time on Loch Morlich beach, our group were called over by Chappy to hear the good news that we were going to try the walk for a second time and hopefully not get lost! We weren't best pleased by this but there was no room for argument and off we trudged into the forest again. This time we were a lot more careful. We got back safely just as the rest were returning from the beach, happy and a bit sunburnt.

Our week at Loch Morlich was to be quite idyllic, giving us plenty of time to bond and to discuss our different options for the future. It would be the last time for many years that I would see my Lawside school friends together, and indeed it was the last time I ever saw quite a number of them. That school trip was unforgettable, particularly because it marked the end of the first part of my life.

In mid-June of 1971, just after my return from Loch Morlich, I persuaded Joe to let me come over to visit him at university. I'd recently attended a "taster" overnight stay with Charlie Maclean at the new Stirling University Campus and we'd had a fantastic time charming two Geordie lasses with our tales of belonging to the elite "Sanny" clan in Scotland, a tribe who only ever wore sandshoes. This gave me a real idea of the fun I might have at university, so I naturally turned to my own brother to draw on his wider knowledge.

That year, Joe and about a dozen of his fellow students were living the bohemian life in Crail Castle, ten miles east of St. Andrews, and not an awful lot of serious studying was going on. Joe was also lucky because his room had French windows that looked out to the lawn, clifftop tower and North Sea beyond. Interestingly, when I went over to visit him, I noticed that the whole castle smelled faintly of cannabis and the students seemed to live entirely on cigarettes, pasta and large trays of scones. These scones were provided for free to "her boys" by the lovely old housekeeper Mrs. Murdoch. Oh, I nearly forgot: there was alcohol too!

The castle's wine cellar was unfortunately empty so the students had converted it into a kind of Gothic discotheque. Joe had painted huge portraits of Jimi Hendrix, Bob Marley and Mick Jagger on the walls and there was a very, very loud sound system in the corner. Upstairs in the huge lounge, there was a grand piano on which a Jewish lad called Andy could recreate the latest tunes of the up-and-coming Elton John. Various musicians would bring along their instruments to the lounge for long jam sessions, with my brother as lead vocalist, and many of his first songs were recorded on reel-to-reel tape right there in that room. Above all however, Crail Castle was a wonderful venue for wild parties and I was led to believe that there were always interesting young ladies hanging around with the boys. I just had to go and see for myself.

Having taken a very long bus ride over to Crail from Dundee (visiting every village in Fife, it seemed) I spent most of that particular Saturday wandering around the castle confirming all that Joe had described to me. There was little or no food, it was freezing cold and most of the residents were sleeping, but the atmosphere slowly began to change as more and more came back to life. Soon there was a serious party brewing. After a few drinks and some casual conversation with a girl wearing a headband and an afghan coat, I was bold enough to persuade a guy called Robbie to sell me a cube of Acid, which was what they all called L.S.D. Robbie was a contemporary of Joe's from Lawside Academy and it seemed he was always enhancing his student loan as a part-time provider of Substances.

Dougie Reid and some others of my wilder pals in Dundee had been taking the drug on and off for quite a while, but I had always resisted the supposed mind-bending trip produced by L.S.D. I had however sometimes enjoyed the calming effects of marijuana. So, deciding that I had to try this experience just one time, with a bit of trepidation I swallowed the cube. Joe was furious when I told him what I'd done, as he'd warned his pals not to give me anything psychedelic, thinking I was too young and having nursed friends through bad times on drugs already. This upset me too, and I said I didn't want to do it anymore, but of course it was too late.

A little later, I looked out of the castle window and saw a French fishing village, complete with 'Onion Johnnie' in beret and stripy top on the quayside, and I was unperturbed, as was the case when I walked through the poster of Stonehenge and waved back to the partygoers in the lounge. I got fed up with apparent hours of Led Zeppelin's "*Moby Dick*" bass riff and drum solo blaring in my ears, took it off the turntable and put it back in its sleeve, and I didn't worry when Robbie told me the record-player had already been switched off for ages. But when I looked down into the room from the corner of the ceiling and saw myself slumped in an old armchair, I decided that this was enough hallucinating to last me a lifetime. So I went outside and stood and spoke to the lampposts for a long time until the weird effects wore off. The next day I took that long bus journey home to Dundee in time for six o'clock mass at the Cathedral. I prayed to be spared flashbacks.

A week later, at home with Mum and Dad and with my last days of schooling at Lawside Academy beckoning, I considered the revels of my night in Crail Castle. I concluded that, although a lifestyle of sex, drugs and rock 'n' roll was undoubtedly available at university, it probably wasn't for me, given my background and upbringing.

I decided that, when I wasn't studying, I'd just concentrate on the sex and rock 'n' roll.

THE END

Also by the author:

Wee Georgie

(Growing up in Dundee in the 50s and 60s)

ISBN 978-0-9927889-1-9

Socrates, the Sprinting Snail of Sorrento

(An illustrated children's book for ages 5-12)

ISBN 978-0-9927889-0-2

Website

www.socratesthesnail.co.uk

44694185R00186

Made in the USA
Middletown, DE
09 May 2019